Marjorie,
"May God give
you many happy
moments on your
of life. God bl
Jean

Life's Struggles
Life's Joys

Experiencing
The Journey of Life

Jean L. Gore

Life's Struggles Life's Joys

Experiencing The Journey of Life

Jean L. Gore

Copyright © 2000
All Rights Reserved

Scripture references from the Revised Standard Version.

PUBLISHED BY:
BRENTWOOD CHRISTIAN PRESS
4000 BEALLWOOD AVENUE
COLUMBUS, GEORGIA 31904

Dedication

To Catherine and Sarah
Grandchildren bring
special joy to life's journey!

Acknowledgements

Initially, I had no thoughts of writing a book. I simply wanted to write something to share at a Christmas luncheon (see "Christmas Joy"). Then, I wrote a poem for one special occasion, and then another, and then even another. Friends started to encourage me to put my writings together into a book. Special friends – like Janice Holden, who would share an experience with me and then wonder out loud if I would write a poem about the experience. She shared the things I wrote with her sister, Jane Huffman, and their mother, Hazeltine Cates, and they joined her in supporting me.

Then there was another friend who encouraged me. Marie Gross has such a sensitive heart. At times, she would read something new that I had written, and tears would come to her eyes as it reminded her of God's love for her. Whenever that happened, I felt that perhaps my writings could touch someone's heart. What an encouragement that was!

Jane Bateman, an excellent Christian speaker and dear friend, is very familiar with Christian books and urged me to keep writing. She also shared my excitement as my book began to take form.

Pastor Larry Bateman not only helped me in my Christian growth as my pastor. He also took the time to review some of what I wrote in order to help my book stay consistent with the truths of God's Word. Rev. Herb Holton also helped with some of the reviewing.

Keith Barrale worked with me in designing a cover for my book and with providing the needed photography. The picture includes the Family Bible that belonged to my husband's grandparents.

My husband, Steve, and our three children, Jennifer, Kimberly, and Stephen, patiently read every word I wrote (not that they had a choice!). More importantly, they believed in me. They had faith that I could finish my book, even when I thought I never would.

Most of all, the Lord helped me so much. He gave me the needed thoughts and words. He gave me opportunities and opened doors that allowed my dream of this book to become a reality. He gave me the gift of life that started me on my own journey, has walked with me on my journey, and, in love, He gave me Himself on a cross, that my journey will one day take me to my final destination – Heaven.

Contents

	Page
LIFE - *A Journey Begins*	9

    A Wonderful Son 10
    His Most Precious Gift 12

MARRIAGE - *A Journey Shared* 13

    A New Tapestry 14
    The Secret of Having a Submissive Wife 15
    A Man to Love 17

LIFE'S STRUGGLES, LIFE'S JOYS -
A Journey's Experiences 19

    Life's Struggles, Life's Joys 20
    Road Sign 22

As Journeys Cross 23
    Fruit Inspection 24
    A Good Man 27
    When I Look At You 29
    Lord, Give Her Love 31
    Road Sign 33
    I Tried to Love 34
    Road Sign 37
    How Much? 38
    No One Knows 40
    Storms of Life 43
    Road Sign 45
    Lost Sheep 46

A Journey With God 49
    Shadows of Doubt 50
    Road Sign 53

Life is a Journey	54
Road Sign	55
The Artist	56
Follow Me	59
Judge God?	63
Road Sign	64
Focus	65
Road Sign	66
Excuses	67
And He Waits	70
Road Sign	72
He Already Knows	73
Road Sign	75
Undeserving	76
Road Sign	78
Still Before You	79
Road Sign	80
So Special	81
Roses	83
Into His Eyes	85
The Present	87
He Seeks Us In So Many Ways	90
Road Sign	92
The Shell and the Sand Dollar	93
Road Sign	96
You Can Praise	97
Reflections	99

DEATH - *A Journey Ends* 103

Ending Before Beginning 104
   A Chance to Live 105
   A New Life 107
   Encounter With A Stranger 108
A Journey Completed 110
   The Beginning of a New Life 111

    There's So Much More 112
    In Your Hands 114
    Last Goodbye 116
    My Husband 118
    My Wife 120
    Road Sign 122
    Why? 123

HEAVEN OR HELL - *After the Journey* 127

Heaven 128
    Road Sign 129
    The Contents of Heaven 130
    Road Sign 132
    Tears In Heaven 133
    Left Alone 136
Hell 139
    The Eternity of Hell 140

SPECIAL DAYS - *God-Given Rest Stops for the Journey* . . 143

Lord's Supper 144
    This Is My Body 145
Easter 147
    Upon That Cross 148
    Thoughts on Easter 149
    A Letter to My Father 152
Thanksgiving 154
    Give Thanks 155
Christmas 157
    The Joy of Christmas 158
    No Christmas Day 160

EPILOGUE – *Road Map to Heaven* 163

LIFE

A Journey Begins

The journey of life begins as a gift, for life is a gift from God. What we do with that gift can often reflect what we feel about the One who gave us that gift. The journey of life has its ups and downs. But through it all, we are never alone.

A Wonderful Son

Your mommy and daddy had so much love
They wanted to share so they asked God above
To send them a baby, a bundle of joy
He answered their prayers with a sweet little boy.

In creating you, God looked around
For the brightest stars that could be found.
He wanted your eyes to twinkle bright
With a radiant glow of heaven's own light.

An angel kissed your mouth so sweet
To give a smile to all you'll meet.
A smile to fill your parents' hearts
With so much joy right from the start.

He formed your hands and your feet too
Thinking of all the things you'll do.
Holding a rattle, throwing a ball
One day walking big and tall.

He gave you a voice to laugh and coo
For learning words like "I love you".
For thanking God for all He'd done
When He gave your parents a wonderful son.

He breathed life in you as only God can
Then gently laid you in your parents' hands.
He gave you to them cause He knew that they
Would raise you in His appointed way.

He'll always be right by your side
To give you protection and be your guide.
May your life be filled with love
You're a special gift from God above.

Let your father and mother be glad, let her who bore you rejoice. Proverbs 23:25

His Most Precious Gift

God gives to us so many gifts
Some gifts are great, some small
But a little one to hold and love
His most precious gift of all.

He gives this gift in many ways
Which way is His to choose
No matter how this gift may come
It's special and brand new.

A brand new life may come to some
By the miracle of birth
Others through adoption
The greatest gift on earth.

For every single little child
Be it girl or boy
Deserves to feel the warmth of love
To experience true joy.

Whoever receives this child in My name receives Me, and whoever receives Me receives Him who sent Me . . . Luke 9:48

MARRIAGE

A Journey Shared

While some people travel their journey of life alone, others share their journey with a marriage partner. In marriage, God can bring the lives of two people together and weave them into a beautiful tapestry. However, this can only happen if both people will allow Him to be not only a part of their marriage, but the head of it.

A New Tapestry

God has brought you both together
As part of His great plan
Your destinies have both been formed
By His own loving hand.

Each life a unique tapestry
Woven by God above
Now He joins them into one
With thread made of His love.

The hem of this new tapestry
He'll form from all your prayers
Submit your lives together to
The Weaver's tender care.

For this reason a man shall leave his father and mother and be joined to his wife, and the two shall become one flesh. Matthew 19:5

The Secret of Having a Submissive Wife

Men read in the Bible that wives are to be
Submissive, and think "That sounds good to me"
They then tell their wives "You must do as I say"
Let me tell you husbands of a much better way.

The first step in having a submissive wife
Is to take a long look at how you live your life
Are you being the man God wants you to be?
Living your life for Him faithfully?

Is it fair to expect her to always obey
If she cannot trust every word that you say?
Your word must be true in things big and small
Or she will never trust you at all.

Do you provide your wife the best that you can
Working together in all of your plans?
Are you willing to sacrifice if you must
To be sure you will always have her trust?

(Continued)

Do you make sure she feels safe and secure?
That's something you must really ensure.
Does she know on you she can depend?
Do you try to be her closest friend?

Do your actions show her just how you feel
That your love for her is strong and real?
When she is hurting are you always there
To provide her with needed love and care?

For this is how Christ treats His very own
Never leaving them feeling lost and alone.
His love is faithful, unselfish and true
As a husband He expects no less from you.

When your wife feels cherished, loved and secure
Her love for you will surely endure
Her being submissive will come easily
When you are the man God wants you to be.

Husbands, love your wives, as Christ loved the church and gave Himself for her. Ephesians 5:25

A Man to Love

A long time ago God gave to me
A very special opportunity
For I met a man and I became his wife
A man to love the rest of my life.

I dreamed of days of endless joy
Of children we'd have, a girl or a boy
A perfect marriage ours would be
A wonderful husband to take care of me.

But I soon learned, to my dismay
That he sometimes wanted things his way
And he soon learned how hard it can be
To understand a wife like me.

For I'm a romantic, as most women are
I like to take walks under the stars
Snuggle together by the fireplace
Kisses planted all over my face.

But he is a man who would rather play
His favorite sport each and every day
Forget romance, for he'd rather be
A man of pure practicality.

As we traveled down life's winding road
We began to carry one another's load
We talked a lot and learned to share
Our joys, our troubles, and our cares.

(Continued)

Walking each day side by side
He taught me how to take life in stride
To worry less and to laugh much more
Isn't that what a husband is for?

Slowly he came to understand
What I really needed from this special man
Was to simply be held in his loving arms
Keeping me safe from every harm.

He makes me feel very loved indeed
As he tries to meet my every need
It's the little things that mean so much
A loving word, a tender touch.

Our lives have had some ups and downs
But through them all we both have found
It takes work and love for marriage to be
All that God intends it to be.

What a blessing it is to be able to live
With a man to whom you want to give
Your love, your dreams, the best part of your life
Forever proud to be his wife.

A long time ago God gave to me
A very special opportunity
Every day I give thanks to God up above
For my special husband, the man I love.

Let each one of you love his wife as himself, and let the wife see that she respects her husband. Ephesians 5:33

LIFE'S STRUGGLES, LIFE'S JOYS
A Journey's Experiences

Our lives resemble a trip across our country. At times, we will travel through valleys of green grass, splashing brooks, and soothing breezes. Although we may long to remain, our journey will take us on. Long stretches of dry desert will spread out before us, but we must go on. Swirling rivers will threaten to end our journey, but a way across will be provided, if we'll just seek it. There will be majestic mountains to climb. Once we reach the top and take in the view around us, we will long to return again and again to life's summits, as if we are trying to get closer to heaven itself. The journey can be a little easier, a little nicer if we will let God go with us and be our guide.

Life's Struggles, Life's Joys

Life isn't fair.

Our lives are all filled with struggles, and with joys. Some people seem to have more of one and less of the other. Whichever one they have more of, it seems they got more of what they don't deserve. The caring, giving people so often seem to suffer the most, while the selfish, greedy people continue to get more and more of the good things of life.

Or so it seems.

Have you ever heard it said of people who love going to garage sales, that "One person's trash is another person's treasure"? I have seen people (and I've been one of them at times) who have all they need and complain because they don't get all they want. I've seen other people (the ones I wish I was more like) who have lost a part of their lives, be it a spouse, a physical ability, their health, or any of the things most of us take for granted. In spite of their difficulties, they still live every minute of life to the fullest and are the happiest people I've ever seen. They find so much pleasure in watching a sunset. They take time to share a smile. They remember to be thankful for the things they do have. It's almost as if they went to the garage sale of life and found as their treasure the things that the rest of us saw as having little value and carelessly discarded.

Am I throwing away treasures?

Do we spend so much of our time nurturing our struggles that our joys are starting to wilt? How can life's most beautiful flowers of joy grow and bloom if we keep letting the weeds of worry choke them out? Are our too often cried tears drowning out the seedlings of happiness? Perhaps it's time to let the Gardener of Life come do some work on the overgrown, unkempt gardens of our lives.

Bouquets

God fills His Heaven with beautiful bouquets. Some are a single white rose bud of a baby's life, cradled in the fern of a grieving parent's love. Others are cheerful buttercups of childhood, filling Heaven with bright, laughing color. Then there are those bouquets full of a variety of the blooming flowers of life's joyful experiences, accented with the stark contrasts of the struggles of life. Each bouquet is lovingly selected and the arrangement specially designed by the Heavenly Florist's own hand. One day we will see how God has arranged all of these bouquets into a beautiful place where we can walk eternally with each other and with Him.

But life is still unfair.

Yes, it is. Children suffer and die. The innocent are victims. Pain and death, hate and cruelty, unfairness and injustice still touch our lives, no matter how hard we try to avoid it all. Even knowing Heaven awaits us one day isn't always enough to get us through all the difficulties, for we see Heaven as then, not now; a distant tomorrow, not today. But the One who is in that distant tomorrow, planning, preparing, and waiting for us to arrive, who was also in yesterday, bleeding, dying, forgiving, is the One who is here today, helping you through all of life's struggles, sharing with you in all of life's joys, but most wonderfully of all, loving you.

For God so loved the world, that He gave His only begotten Son, that whosoever believeth in Him shall have everlasting life. John 3:16

Road Sign

If we were truly honest about it, wouldn't we admit that our blessings outnumber our tears? If not, then maybe we're spending too much time counting the wrong thing.

> Our job is to count the blessings.
> God's job is to count the tears.

As Journeys Cross

We each have our own journey. But no journey, no matter how long or how short, is traveled without crossing other people's journeys. Sometimes we travel together for a while. When we do, some journeys are made easier, while others are slowed down or even detoured. If you come across someone broke down on their journey, are you willing to stop and help them? Are you willing to accept their help when you get stalled? Do you push others out of your way, or let their journey merge with yours for a while? What kind of driver in the journey of life are you?

Fruit Inspection

Most of us have had this experience at one time or another. You open the refrigerator door and something just doesn't smell quite right. You start searching. You look behind the pitcher of tea and the bottles of soda - nothing offensive there. You check inside a few covered bowls - everything still appears to be edible. Finally, you open one of the bottom drawers and take three steps backwards - you've found the offending odor! A peek inside reveals a piece of fruit that looks as if it might have been an orange a few weeks ago. Yes, there are still places around the brown areas that still resemble the skin of an orange. You call someone else over and point out to them how disgusting this piece of fruit has become. You both agree that it is simply horrible and that this disgusting piece of fruit simply has to go. You reach for several paper towels and a plastic bag. You carefully pick up this soft, squishy piece of fruit and quickly drop it into the bag. Holding it at arms length, and trying not to breathe too deeply, you carry it outside and dispose of it in the trash can. Returning to the kitchen, you open a window and begin scrubbing out that refrigerator drawer.

People are much like fruit. Some can be just as sweet as a fresh, juicy apple. Others who have been left out in the world too long have started developing some bad spots, just like that orange did. These spots may be pride, self-centeredness, unkindness, or any other variety of what we generally call sin. Some people look perfectly fine from where you stand, but as you get to know them better, you find they too have their bad spots. Some of them may be hidden underneath, or they may be starting inside, just like an apple that has a worm in it but you don't know it's there until you cut into it. Other people are like that piece of fruit inside the refrigerator - the problems are so obvious that we become aware of them even from a distance.

When we find a person who has started to "go bad", much like a spoiling piece of fruit, there are many different ways that we choose to handle him. Often, we call someone else and point out this person's faults and then we discuss what to do about him. We may try to distance ourselves from him. After all, we wouldn't want any of that offensive odor to get on us. Perhaps we decide to try to get rid of this bad piece of fruit by excluding him from our group of friends. If we're in a situation where we can't get away from him, then we can always be cold towards him and pretend that he doesn't exist. We can tell everyone we know about him and ask them to join us in prayer in order to tell God exactly what is wrong with this person and how He needs to either clean this person up or get him out of our lives. Of course, after saying that kind of prayer, we would want to walk quickly away before God gets a chance to tell us that He also needs to do a little "cleaning up" with us too (unless we'd prefer that God remove us from *His* life). Some of us like to refer to all of this as "fruit inspection" rather than admit that we've crossed the line into "judging" (which God frowns on just as much, if not more, than what has caused that person to "go bad").

Now, let's imagine what our Lord would do with a person who has become a "spoiled piece of fruit" (which is actually every single one of us). First, provided that person is willing, He would gently pick him up with His own hands. The offensive look and smell would never get in His way of helping, nor would He ever hold the person at arm's length. He would then carry the person to His Father, and allow Him to make the determination of whether this person should be "thrown in the trash" or transformed into the wonderful person that God intended him to be all along. Of course, God never throws anyone away. The only ones who will ever be eventually thrown out are those who refuse to allow Jesus to carry him to God for renewal.

We, too, can follow Jesus' example. When we meet someone who we find offensive in some way, or that we notice is not living as God taught us to live, we can have compassion for that person. We don't need to embarrass that person by informing everyone we know how bad that person has become. Instead, we can pick them up with the gentle hands of prayer and carry him to our Father. Knowing of the transforming work

God has been performing in our own lives, and knowing that God alone knows what needs to be done to restore this person, we can leave him in His strong, capable hands without any advice from us about how to do the job. We may want to stand by and be ready if God decides to honor us by involving us in carrying out His miracle (although He can easily do it without us). Some people may rightly call this "fruit inspection". I simply prefer to call it "the fruit of love".

But the fruit of the Spirit is love, joy, peace patience, kindness, goodness, faithfulness, gentleness, self-control. Galatians 5:22-23

A Good Man

I don't know much about you
Or what's happened in your life
About the joys and sorrows
The excitement and the strife

I don't know what your dreams are
For the remainder of your years
What puts a smile upon your face
Or prompts a single tear

But I know you are a good man
and that your word is true
I know you strive to do your best
In everything you do

I know that you are a smart man
Evident by books that you read
I know you are a caring man
That's shown by your loving deeds

(Continued)

I know you are a gentle man
Treating each one with respect
I know you are a brave man
Your loved ones you protect

I know that you are a fair man
At work you're often praised
I know you are a loving man
By the family that you raised

I know you're not a perfect man
You have your faults, though few
I also have my own faults
Therefore I can't judge you

I know that most importantly
You belong to God above
You are the apple of His eye
The object of His love

Lead a life worthy of the Lord, fully pleasing to Him, bearing fruit in every good work and increasing in the knowledge of God. Colossians 1:10

When I Look At You

When I look at you I see someone
Who cares how others feel
What you do is from your heart
Your love for them is real.

When I look at you I see someone
Who cares about what you do
You give your all in everything
Big jobs and small ones too.

When I look at you I see someone
Who helps out whenever you can
Never held back by other's words
Nor afraid to take a stand.

When I look at you I see someone
Who has a joyful heart
No matter how bad it all may seem
To others joy you impart.

(Continued)

When I look at you I see someone
Who tries to do her best
No matter how hard the job may be
You always meet the test.

When I look at you I see someone
Who has a heart of gold
You've found the fabled fountain of youth
Your spirit will never grow old.

When I look at you I see someone
With such a lovely face
The glow of love within your soul
Can brighten any place.

When I look at you I see someone
Who loves the Lord above
Your life is ever a testimony
Of His unending love.

Wherefore, my beloved brethren, be steadfast, immovable, always abounding in the work of the Lord, knowing that in the Lord your labour is not in vain. 1 Corinthians 15:58

Lord, Give Her Love

She has burdens to bear
and crosses to carry.
Trials that make
her heart feel heavy
Lord, give her strength.

She has clouds in her sky
that darken her way.
And paths that seem
uphill all the way.
Lord, give her hope.

She has worries and cares
that weigh her down.
She tries so hard
not to frown.
Lord, give her peace.

She has sorrow and pain
no one else can know.
They've no idea what
she must undergo.
Lord, give her comfort.

(Continued)

She has sadness and griefs
that break her heart.
Life has been rough
right from the start.
Lord, give her joy.

She has family who all
make demands on her time.
Into her lap her
grandchildren climb.
Lord, give her patience.

She has a need for You
deep down in her soul.
Only You can make
her spirit whole.
Lord, give her love.

May you be strengthened with all power, according to His glorious might, for all endurance and patience. Colossians 1:11

Road Sign

When we are driving down the road, we periodically glance in our rearview mirror to see what is behind us. Sometimes, we need to move over if there is a faster vehicle about to run over us, or there is an emergency vehicle that needs to go past. However, we can only afford glances. The only time we look in the rearview mirror for any length of time is when we are moving backwards.

On our journey through life, it is important to glance in the rearview mirror at our past. Some of our past experiences may be threatening our journey. Something urgent may still need to be taken care of. However, if we spend most of our time looking in that rearview mirror, it will make moving forward a lot more difficult. Remember which way you are traveling. Keep your main focus on your destination.

I Tried to Love

I tried to love those around me
But it seemed I was doing it wrong
No matter how much I tried to love
It seemed I didn't belong.

I tried to love those around me
And change them for the good
But they continued to do as they pleased
Though I tried as hard as I could.

I tried to love those around me
But it was not easy to do
For some people are so unlikeable
Disrespectful and arrogant too.

I tried to love those around me
But was called fool and other names
For others just took advantage of me
I figured that I was to blame.

I tried to love those around me
But the task just seemed too great
I was ready to quit, simply give up
But Jesus said "Child, wait.

You tried to love those around you
But you were doing it wrong
You loved for what you could get in return
And only felt you didn't belong.

You tried to love those around you
And tried as hard as you could
But love is accepting, not changing
Love only looks for the good.

You tried to love those around you
But found it was not easy to do
But their arrogance is really their hurt
Disrespect is their fear of you.

You tried to love those around you
And was called fool and other names
I know how deeply it hurt you
For I have been called the same.

You tried to love those around you
But the task just seemed too great
You tried to love them all on your own
Not letting Me carry the weight.

(Continued)

I commanded you 'Love those around you'
With no promise of love in return
For they find it hard to understand
And often respond with scorn.

I commanded you 'Love those around you'
But conditions I did not give
Love hinges not on the way that they act
Nor how they may choose to live.

I commanded you 'Love those around you'
But I knew you couldn't do it yourself
So I sent you a Helper to show you the way
If you will just ask Him to help.

I commanded you 'Love those around you'
I knew what the cost would be
But I've never asked you to pay as much
As I did on Calvary's tree.

I commanded you 'Love those around you'
It's really not so hard to do
Just look at others through My caring eyes
And love them as I have loved you."

A new commandment I give to you, that you love one another, even as I have loved you, that you also love one another. John 13:34

Road Sign

We sometimes think that God wants us to obey Him in order to have His needs met.

We need to remember that the all-sufficient God has no need.

Perhaps then we will begin to realize just whose needs He's trying to meet.

How Much?

How much would we want God to love each of us
If He loved as we do, would we all then fuss
Noticing us only on Christmas day
The rest of the year simply turning away?

Would He just call us when He has a need
Then turn a deaf ear when to Him we would plead
After we've done what He's asked us to do
Would He turn away without a "thank you"?

Would He just assume we've no need of Him
Only talking to us when He has a whim?
No that's not the way God loves you and me
For His love's everywhere for us all to see.

Just look around and behold how it grows
In a strong, tall oak tree, or a delicate rose
His love is above us in the stars twinkling bright
And it shines down upon us in the sun's warmth and light.

His love wraps around us in springtime's soft breeze
And flutters about us in fall's vibrant leaves
His love touches us with a sweet tenderness
As it moves all around us in the warm wind's caress.

It lifts up our spirits with the birds on the wing
And fills our hearts with the song those birds sing
In the roaring thunder is the sound of its power
It's gentleness found in the cool evening shower.

Lightening writes His love in the sky
He whispers it softly in a baby's first cry.
God's love was not given without sacrifice
The life of His Son, a very dear price.

His love shines forth brightly from an old rugged cross
Reaching through time to a world that is lost
Oh how He longs to make all of us His
And show each of us what love really is.

God does not love the way that we do
For His love is unchanging, eternal and true
His love always was and ever will be
That is how much God loves you and me.

God shows His love for us in that while we were yet sinners Christ died for us. Romans 5:8

No One Knows

There's a part of me that no one knows
I keep it hid away
For if others saw this part of me
I don't know what they'd say.

I must be strong, my head held high
They must not see the tears
I have to act like nothing's wrong
They must not see the fears.

Sometimes I even fool myself
That everything's all right
But that can be so hard to do
In the middle of the night.

That is the time I think about
All that I've been through
Sometimes I fear this pain inside
Will break my heart in two.

I try to push away the thoughts
Of all my past regrets
I cannot change them anyway
I just wish I could forget.

Sometimes I think of family
Who years ago have died.
And fight to hold back unshed tears
The ones I've never cried.

Oh dear Lord, what's wrong with me
I was not raised this way
I'm not supposed to feel like this
At least, that's what they say.

How I wish that just one time
I could just be me
Share my pain with someone else
Accept their sympathy.

Or let them see how really scared
I am of what's ahead
No, I must not let them see
I must be brave instead.

My dear child it breaks My heart
To see you suffer so.
For pain and fear are part of life
Feelings all must know.

(Continued)

It was not part of My great plan
For you to bear alone
All the pain and trials of life
Your heart's not made of stone.

If you'll just reach outside yourself
To those who really care
Let them see you as you are
Your troubles you can share.

You can help each other bear
The burden of your load
Hand in hand both walking down
Life's long uncertain road.

Be not afraid to share your tears
My example to accept
For in My word it's written down
That even Jesus wept.

Bear one another's burdens, and so fulfill the law of Christ. Galatians 6:2

Storms of Life

Did you grow up in a dark and cold existence? Was the inner depths of the storm your home? Does the following feel familiar? Perhaps, you are still living within the storm.

All around you, the storms continue to rage. Stinging winds of disapproving words whip around you, wearing you down. There are icy stares of rejection, their sharp points piercing your heart. The bitter cold of feeling unloved penetrates your very being. The darkness of empty promises surrounds you. You are tossed about in the darkness by gales of confusion. Neglect rains upon you, drowning your roots. Loud voices of humiliation thunder around you. The lightening streaks of anxiety cross your darkness. The hail of despair beats you down. The flood of fear covers you. Your every step seems to be followed by a black cloud of sadness. Each day's forecast feels like one of continued hopelessness.

Has your inner being become frozen by the cold so that a solid cold center still remains within you. Others have tried to warm it with their love, but it lies too deep for them to reach. The light of hope cannot seem to penetrate the remaining darkness. Your flooded roots have yet to grow deep and strong, leaving you unsteady and unsure. The wounds from the stinging winds have left you exposed and vulnerable. The gales have left you lost and wandering. There remains a trembling within you from a storm too long endured. The onslaughts of hail have left you bent and bruised. At times, the flood of fear still threatens to take you under once more.

Heaven looks down in love and compassion on the broken and weary. Just as Jesus calmed the storm that was causing the disciples such distress and fear, He also longs to stretch forth His hands out over your life and again say, "Peace, be still". The lightening strikes of anxiety will start to fade. The echoes of the thunder will begin to be silenced. A warm, soft shower of healing will soothe the pain. The sunshine of His love, shining through the shower of healing, will create a rainbow of hope within you. The warmth of His love will penetrate to the very depths of you, gradually melting away all remaining fingers of ice from around your heart and soul. He wants to invite you to send your roots deep into His Word that holds ever strong. When more squalls come, He will walk across the turbulent waves to you and you will never have to face life's storms alone.

The changes won't come over night. It's a lifelong process. Sometimes we resist His help. We mistake His showers of healing for the rain of neglect we have become used to. We close our eyes to the brightness of His love that we are unaccustomed to. We are afraid to trust the rainbow of hope, fearing that it will somehow fade into the familiar empty darkness that remains from promises broken. We allow our roots to remain in the stagnant pool of past pain, fed only with present hurts, rather than plant them in the stability and nourishment of God's truths. When the squalls come again, we run in fear for we have not yet learned to look for Him walking toward us on the troubled waves.

I know you are tired, hurting, weak, and afraid. You don't know if you can try any more. The fog left over from the storm you endured envelopes you, making Him hard to see and His voice sound muffled. You don't have the strength to reach out very far. But, if you'll reach out just a little, you'll find that He is closer than you think. Reach out with your arms, placing them around His neck. He will lift you up, cradling you close to His chest. His hand will tenderly wipe the tears from your eyes and the pain from your heart. Look into His eyes. No matter what anyone has ever told you, He loves you. No matter what may have happened to you, He loves you. No matter what you may have done, He loves you - not because of who your are or what you have accomplished, but because of who He is. No one in your life can come between you and His dear look of love. He won't allow it. Close your eyes, lay your head on His shoulder, and let Him calm the storm and begin His healing in you.

Thou are a hiding place for me, Thou preservest me from trouble. Psalms 32:7

Road Sign

We'd rather hold on to the certainty of the known, than reach for the uncertainty of the unknown that God is trying to guide us to;

Even though the One who gives us all is the greatest certainty there is.

Lost Sheep

Oh Lord how I have longed
To bring lost sheep to Thee
Some have strayed down paths
Where they shouldn't be.

They need Your gentle voice
To guide them on their way
To pastures fresh and sweet
Where they can rest and play.

Many sheep have fallen
Down lonely, steep hillsides
If I listen really closely
I can hear their cries.

You reach down with Your staff
And lift them to Your arms
Returning them to Your fold
Where they are safe from harm.

There are hungry wolves
Who make little lambs their prey
But Your rod You swiftly throw
And scare the wolves away.

But Dear Lord, I have failed
I've not traveled far at all
No foreign soil have trod
In following Your call.

I have not ventured out
To some far and distant land
To find the lost sheep there
And guide them to Your hand.

How many little lambs
Could I have brought to Thee
If only Your soft voice
I'd followed faithfully.

Instead I stayed behind
To raise my family
I let others go ahead
And do the job for me.

Then the Lord looked down
With love and sympathy
And said to me, "My child,
You did not fail Me.

All I ever asked
Was for a willing heart
And that you truly had
I saw it from the start.

Perhaps you cannot go
To lands across the sea
But you can send someone
Together, you'll serve Me.

(Continued)

But many of My sheep
Live right outside your door
And they are just as lost
As those on distant shores.

They do not have to have
Different skin or different eyes.
Some of your closest friends
Are lost sheep in disguise."

Dear Lord, help me to lead
The lost lambs home to Thee
They may live next door
Or far away from me.

Help me to realize
When "into all the world" You send
It may be far away
Or just around the bend.

Oh Lord, how I have longed
To bring lost sheep to Thee
Help me do just this
Wherever I may be.

I have other sheep, that are not of this fold; I must bring them also, and they will heed My voice. So there shall be one flock, one shepherd. John 10:16

A Journey With God

Would you want to take a long, long trip all by yourself? No one to talk to, no one to share the experience with, no one to help you with the driving? God would love to come along on your journey with you. It is a good idea to invite Him along too. After all, He has the map.

Shadows of Doubt

There's a part of me that would like to believe in God. But, then there are all those shadows of doubts being cast around me. I've heard the story of Jesus, but what about all the theories - you know, the ones about evolution, and the Big Bang theory? What of all the psychics and cults? How do I know which religion has the truth? What about all the suffering in the world? I don't want to die, and then find out that I trusted in the wrong thing.

One doubt is cast as some of the scientists want us to believe that we evolved through the years to be what we are today. I look around at all that nature holds - the different trees, plants, flowers; some of the strange looking creatures from the sea; the insects that burrow beneath the ground or buzz through the air; the tiny hummingbird and the soaring eagle; the various species from the animal kingdom; and man himself, each person with his own unique set of fingerprints. I'm supposed to believe that all of this came about, including myself, from chance? If life evolves to higher levels based on survival of the fittest, why would it evolve to a point where that life would be on the verge of destroying it all?

If we are to believe that life evolved from a lifeless ball of matter spinning in space, where did that ball called earth come from? Could it be possible that all matter in the universe was once compressed into one small area, and then exploded to become the universe? Even if that did happen, where would the compressed matter come from and what would cause it to explode into a universe with a solar system and an earth that would contain the necessary gasses to evolve into a life form that could feel, reason, hate, love?

Could life really exist without an ever present, all powerful, all knowing God to think of it and create it and sustain it?

Another doubt is cast as more and more I hear of people who are psychics or have special powers to know things and do things beyond what is considered capable of "normal" man. If these people are all fakes, then there is no need to even consider them. If they are not, and if there is a power they can tap into as they describe, then we desperately need a just and righteous God who we can turn to for guidance and protection.

Throughout the history of mankind, in every civilization, there has been evidence of even the most primitive man reaching out to a power, or force, or god beyond themselves. In some ways, their search resembles that of a life just born, instinctively turning to its mother for nourishment, not questioning her existence but simply crying out for her to help sustain its life. Why would man instinctively search for Someone if that Someone does not exist?

With all the various beliefs, how do we know which one is the right one? Each one claims authenticity. Some claim that the Holy Bible is the truth, but how can I be sure? Can the answer be found in another question: has anyone ever disproved it? Many have certainly tried. So far, history and science continue to support the Bible's claims. Those who thought they had found inconsistencies in it have been taken back to the writings in the original languages and those so called inconsistencies ceased to exist. Many men who lived in different areas and hundreds of years apart all gave various accounts in the Bible of a man who would be born in Bethlehem, have certain events happen in His life, and then die unjustly and cruelly. It would be amazing if one man predicted this with such accuracy. But the chances for several men, living in different places and times to tell the future accounts that could be true of only one person and for it all to actually occur as told are unimaginable, and yet, it happened.

So, if the Bible is true, what of all the needless suffering in the world, especially of the innocent? If God is a God of love, why do these things happen? Yet, isn't God supposed to be just and righteous? A God who is perfect in His justice would have to allow his creation to experience the consequences of their actions. Yet, this God of love and mercy instead took those consequences on Himself in order to spare us. If He never did anything else for us, never provide one miracle, one healing, one blessing, He would still be a God of love and mercy, simply because of that one unfathomable act of kindness. Man wants God to leave him alone to live his life as he pleases, but when his actions hurt someone who did not deserve it, then man wants to blame God for not intervening and stopping him. We throw away food while children die of starvation, and we say we can't get involved when distorted or cruel people prey on the defenseless, then we shake our fists in God's face in anger and ask "why?". It's time we accept our own responsibility for what happens around us. God never intended for us to know suffering nor is He to blame. This Bible, that has yet to be disproved, teaches of one who foolishly thought he could be God's equal. The pride of an angel led to rebellion and the birth of evil. As this outcast angel rises up among mankind in an attempt to spread his rebellion to all who will join him, he casts shadows of doubt around us all. But long ago, from a cold dark tomb, rose the Son of God. His holy light of love and hope shines forth through all time, dispelling those disturbing shadows of doubt, and in their place rises the reassuring shadow of a cross - our symbol for love, life and truth.

I believe; help my unbelief. Mark 9:24

Road Sign

When you set out on a trip, and during the trip, there are certain things you have to take care of. You need to start out with plenty of gas, and keep an eye on the gas needle to be sure you don't run out. You need to have enough oil to keep the engine running smoothly. You need the proper antifreeze so your car won't freeze up when you run into some cold weather. You also want to have plenty of washer fluid to help you keep your windshield clean so you can have a clear view ahead of you.

As we continue through life's journey, we need to keep our tanks full of prayer. If we let them run out, we'll start sputtering and slowing down. We need a good supply of God's Word to keep us running smoothly through the ups and downs of life. We need the warmth of fellowship so that our hearts don't freeze up when we travel through some of the dark, cold sections of life. And we need to have an abundance of God's spirit within us to help us have a clear view of where we are headed.

Don't try to run on empty.

Life Is a Journey

Life is a journey, one we all take
Destinations determined by decisions we make
This can be scary, wondering what's best to do
Especially knowing it's not all up to you.

For just when you think you have it all in your hands
Life suddenly hands you situations unplanned
A letter delivered, a call in the night
Where you had planned to go left, you now must go right.

Your orderly world gets turned upside down
Your patience wears thin, your head starts to pound
You think of the past and may even yearn
To familiar paths you once more could return.

But although the past holds memories dear
The future is beckoning you to draw near
For in it you'll find just around the next bend
Excitement and joy and even new friends.

One day you'll look back and then you will see
That life has unfolded as was meant to be
For throughout our life God looks down from above
And guides all our steps with His unfailing love.

The steps of a man are from the Lord, and He establishes him in whose way He delights; though he fall, he shall not be cast headlong, for the Lord is the stay of his hand. Psalms 37:23-24

Road Sign

I'm seeing some of my prayers being answered today
Prayers that were first prayed 30 years ago
Prayers that I didn't think would be answered

"Lord, help me to trust Your timing. Although I couldn't see it or understand as it was happening, You were working with me in a way that would gently begin to mold me into Your image. I see now that if You had answered my prayers back then as I wanted You to, I might have been broken in the process. Thank you for being so patient with my impatience."

The Artist

Can you imagine how an artist would feel
After days with his brush in hand
Carefully sketching the smallest detail
Of the picture he'd already planned.

He filled in the spaces with colors so bright
With soft shading here and there
He finished it with one last careful stroke
A picture that's painted with care.

The next day he comes back anxious to see
The work done with loving hands
But tears fill his eyes as he gazes upon
The picture that sits on his stand.

For the colors have moved from their appointed space
To ones which for them were not planned
And the lines have taken on different shapes
Than those drawn by the artist's own hand.

And what of the potter who sits at his wheel
Molding a new lump of clay
Lovingly shaping it to the right form
That he intended to make that day.

He looks over his work that now stands complete
Satisfied that he did his job well
Gently he places it up on a shelf
With pride his heart starts to swell.

He leaves his new creation a while
Not knowing that when he returns
This beautiful piece that he has made
Will have taken on a new form.

What of the writer who works patiently
With words and paper and pen
Expressing to all who would read his work
Feelings that come from within.

Choosing each word with infinite care
So his meaning is clear to each one
He writes the last line with a satisfied smile
Pleased with the work he has done.

Then reading back through the story he wrote
Disappointment soon fills his heart
For the words have changed and rearranged
A different story right from the start.

How absurd it seems for us to think
How a picture might repaint itself
Or a ceramic piece reshape its form
After being placed on a shelf.

(Continued)

That words could move about on a page
To change how a story might end
But it really isn't all that absurd
It's happened to us, my friend.

We are the picture that was meant to be
A portrait of God up above
Clay molded to be His image so true
A story of God's wondrous love.

But we decided that we'd rather be
The creator instead of the art
So we rearranged, remolded and changed
In the process breaking God's heart.

If we'll place ourselves back into the hands
Of the Artist in Heaven above
He'll repaint and remold us in His image again
Rewriting His story of love.

For we are His workmanship, created in Christ Jesus for good works, which God prepared beforehand, that we should walk in them. Ephesians 2:10

Follow Me

Preface

Often, we have heard the story of how Jesus asked Peter three times if he loved Him. I understood that there was a relation between this question being asked three times and Peter having denied his Lord three times. I had wondered what I would say if the Lord was to ask me if I loved Him enough to die for Him. Did Jesus really expect that much from Peter? Does He expect that much from us today? What if our love doesn't meet the test? How does the Lord see us then?

What a difference it makes when a man of God shares with us the original Greek words and their meaning in order to help us see a lesson more clearly than before. My appreciation goes to Pastor Larry Bateman for being that man and for his sermon that brought this story alive and new for me, and showed me how the Lord does see us when our love for Him doesn't quite measure up to what we would like it to be.

(Pastor Larry Bateman came to be the pastor of Norview Baptist Church in Norfolk VA in the spring of 1997.)

Follow Me

Many days had Peter spent
At His Savior's side
It wasn't many days ago
This dear Savior died.

Although it broke his heart in two
His sadness was short lived
For Peter heard that Christ arose
New life and hope to give.

Though he was glad, he still bore
Such guilt and pain inside
As he remembered those three times
His Savior he denied.

Then one night as Peter fished
He saw Jesus on the shore
He quickly left his boat behind
To be with Him once more.

They shared a meal the Lord had fixed
The disciples gathered near
Especially Peter when Jesus spoke
The words he needed to hear.

"Do you love Me, Peter," Jesus asked
"Enough to die for Me?"
Peter replied "You're my best friend.
This I'm sure you see."

"Then feed My little precious lambs"
The Lord said tenderly
"Tell them of My Father's love
Poured forth at Calvary."

"Do you love Me," Jesus asked again
"Enough to die for Me?"
I care about you very much
Peter answered truthfully.

"Then take care of My flock of sheep
They often go astray.
They need someone to tend to them
I'll show you the way."

"Do you like Me?" Jesus then asked him
"How deep does your love go?"
For Jesus knew it would take time
For Peter's love to grow.

Peter said "You know my heart.
"You are my dearest friend.
Though at times I may fail you,
I'll care until the end."

"Then feed My sheep My precious word"
The Lord commanded him.
"Tell them how I gave My life
To give new life to them."

Three times the Lord asked Peter of
The love he felt inside
Reminding him the way that he
Three times his Lord denied.

Although that must have hurt him so
It could not have compared
To how he felt when to the Lord
His soul he humbly bared.

(Continued)

To tell the One who died for him
He could not do the same
Though Peter cared about the Lord
Deep love he could not claim.

But Jesus knew this dear man's heart
And that he tried his best.
He told Peter "Follow Me,
And I will do the rest."

Do you feel like Peter did
You know your love is small.
You give so little to the Lord
When you want to give Him all.

Do you tell Him honestly
Just how you really feel
Though you cannot give Him all
He knows your love is real.

Just as that day so long ago
The Lord drew Peter near
Jesus speaks the words to you
The ones you need to hear.

For Jesus also knows your heart
Asking only for your best
Hear Him tell you "Follow Me"
And trust Him with the rest.

If any man would come after Me, let him deny himself and take up his cross daily and follow Me. Luke 9:23

Judge God?

Would you criticize God for the things He does
Would you judge His plan, the way that He loves
Do you feel you know so much more than He
Of what is needed by both you and me?

Would you fuss with Him over His Master Plan
Have Him place it all in your human hand
Tell Him what time each thing should be done
Do you think you know more than the Almighty One?

When we carelessly judge our fellowman
Are we not also judging His Master Plan
If we can trust God with our own very soul
Can we not also trust Him to make each of us whole?

Is He not working for the hearts of all men
To redeem each one from the cruel grip of sin
Patiently working year after year
To reach those who live in despair and fear?

When someone goes his own selfish way
Refusing to listen to what God has to say
Ignoring the love shown on Calvary's hill
God still allows man to have his free will.

God works in each life day after day
For those who will let Him have His own way
It may not happen like we think that it should
But remember that God is both wise and good.

Trust in the Lord with all your heart, and do not rely on your own insight. Proverbs 3:5

Road Sign

When the vision of our wants comes into focus with the vision of His wants, then we will have 20/20 spiritual vision.

Focus

Oh Lord I worry so very much
About what others think of me
Instead of focusing solely upon
Approval that comes from Thee.

I want others to give me love
Compromising values to attain
A gift that is changing and unsure
The cost is more than the gain.

That's when I give up the special bond
That You and I have shared
When I put others ahead of You
Forgetting how much You care.

I do things that I will later regret
To obtain their approving smiles
Forgetting that You are watching me
And loving me all the while.

Dear Lord please help me again to know
Deep within my heart
That putting You first will always meet
My needs right from the start.

Help me to keep my heart and mind
Fixed solely on You above
Fill me with Your joy and peace
Sustain me with Your love.

How long will you go limping with two different opinions? If the Lord is God, follow Him. 1 Kings 18:21

Road Sign

It seems easier for us to say "yes" to the world and "no" to God.

Why is it so hard to turn from the things in the world that will ultimately hurt us and accept the things of God that will ultimately give all we need?

Excuses

God has so much for me to do
But I have my life to live
So instead of doing what He wants
Excuses I must give.

The first one that I like to use
Is I can't hear His voice
I say I want to know His will
But not listening is my choice.

I fill my life with so much noise
And busyness each day
That way I'm sure I cannot hear
The words He wants to say.

Sometimes He catches me off guard
I almost change my mind
Then I stop and realize
More excuses I must find.

For if I listen to His voice
And choose freely to obey
My life no more would be my own
To live in my own way.

I tell Him I can't possibly
Do what He asks of me
I can't find the time it takes
To serve Him faithfully.

(Continued)

Even if I found the time
Five minutes here or there
I need that time to meet my needs
Not spend it all in prayer.

Besides, there's nothing I can do
I'm just plain old me
Why does He ask me to do things
When I lack the ability?

Please don't try to tell me how
He'll give me all I need
I don't want to know the truth
Of how faithfully He leads.

I wouldn't mind it quite so much
If these things were lots of fun
If they would bring me wealth and fame
When my work was finally done.

But what He asks is so mundane
Work with no reward
Not something I would want to do
Not even for the Lord.

What if I tried to do these things
If I let Him have His way
People would make fun of me
Think of what they'd say!

They might call me "Christian"
Though that's what I claim to be
But it's meant to be a secret
Not something they can see.

Just let me live my life of ease
I don't want to care
But when God gives out His blessings
Make sure I get my share.

Don't ask me to live for Him
Who gave His life for me.
Don't ask me to respond
With answers honestly.

I don't want to let Him know
(Though He knows it anyway)
That just a selfish life is what
I want to live each day.

You can live your life for Him
Your sacrifices make
In all the things you do for Him
Real pleasure you can take.

But if a shallow, empty life
Is what you want to live
Instead of doing what He wants
Excuses you must give.

Know the God of your father, and serve Him with a whole heart and a willing mind. 1 Chronicles 28:9

And He Waits

Morning comes; we prepare for the day.
So much to do; no time to pray
Our job awaits, responsibilities call
There's not enough time to do it all.
And He waits.

Our children our born; how quickly they grow
No time to tell them that God loves them so
There's school and recitals; ball games to play
Forget church on Sunday, my only free day.
And He still waits.

Easter comes; we again make our way
A yearly visit to church this spring day
A preacher talks of God's love so dear
A sermon I hear, year after year.
And He patiently waits.

We hear of His love and forgiveness from sin
The invitation given to ask the Lord in
I'd be too embarrassed to walk down that aisle
I'll do it later, just give me a while.
And He lovingly waits.

Age creeps up upon me, my health starts to fade
Many trips to the doctor now must be made
One day I still plan to invite Jesus in
As soon as I'm feeling better again.
And He continually waits.

Life is now over; how can this be
I find Heaven's gates are all closed to me
No more chances to invite Him in
I wish I had it to do over again.
For He no longer waits.

The Lord waits to be gracious to you; therefore, He exalts Himself to show mercy to you. Isaiah 30:18

Road Sign

God satisfies all of our wants.

But first, we have to let Him teach us a whole new set of "wants".

He Already Knows

Our prayers are full of formal words
Oft said from bended knees
Words not meant to tell the truth
But simply meant to please.

We try so hard to keep from Him
The way we feel inside
Our selfish and our sinful thoughts
From Him we try to hide.

Perhaps we fear that we will lose
His mercy and His love
The moment that we let Him know
The things we're thinking of.

What punishment would He send down
If we would let Him know
That there are times we go astray
And disappoint Him so?

We long deep down within our souls
His look of love to win
We try to hide from Him the fact
That we're still prone to sin.

(Continued)

It's true that God gets angry with
The things that we do wrong
But His forgiving love for us
Is still both deep and strong.

Besides that, He already knows
What's deep within our hearts
He wants to hear about it all
So healing then can start.

Nothing that we say to Him
Will catch Him by surprise.
He already knows the wrongs we've done
The hate, the pride, the lies.

So open up your heart to Him
You'll find He understands
And He will help you through it all
With His own guiding hand.

We have no need to fear Him now
No matter what we've done
He proved how much He loves us when
He gave us His own Son.

Know the God of your father, and serve Him with a whole heart and with a willing mind; for the Lord searches all hearts, and understands every plan and thought. 1 Chronicles 28:9

Road Sign

If God feels our pain, our rejection, our disappointments, does He also feel it when comfort, acceptance and love is given?

Undeserving

The teenager left the party. He'd had plenty of beer. Joints of marijuana had been passed around. He only had a few blocks to drive in order to get home. He never saw the light change to red. He never noticed the other set of headlights entering the intersection. He didn't remember the sound of the crash. But he'll never forget the dying cries of a young mother.

He waited in the shadows, watching. He slipped quietly behind a man walking home. He pressed the hard end of a gun into the man's back and demanded money. He tore the watch from the man's arm. He even took the simple wedding ring the man had worn for over forty years. He stuffed it all in his pockets, enough to feed his drug habit one more day.

The little girl was pretty in her pale blue dress. Blond curls framed a delicate face. Heavy make up barely concealed the bruise on the side of her head. The white roses on the casket were in stark contrast to the brutality of the way a young life was ended at the hands of an out-of-control, abusive parent.

As the sun began to set, darkness filled the room. A frail, wrinkled hand reached out to turn on a light. The room was turning cold. As the elderly woman struggled to get up from her bed, the night air met her gown, damp with urine, and a chill went through her. Painful, slow steps took her to the kitchen. All that waited for her there was some dry cereal and a glass of water. In the hall hung a family portrait - a portrait of people who were once her children, whom she lovingly tended to - a portrait of people who had since become strangers to her, who no longer cared what happened to her.

Throughout the city, the remnants of bombed buildings continued to burn. Smoke darkened the sky. In the distance, gunfire could still be heard above the cries of now orphaned children. The smell of death lingered heavily on the night air. The wounded soldier wandered around the lifeless bodies, dazed by the senseless destruction of war.

It was mid-afternoon. Sweat trickled down His face, burned His eyes. His chest barely moved in shallow breaths. Pain kept Him from breathing any deeper. The ache in His shoulders and back was almost unbearable. The bitter taste of vinegar lingered on his parched lips. Finally, it was finished. Mankind had taken the life of God's own Son.

God, why do you love us so, when we are so undeserving? What would become of us if You didn't?

The Lord is merciful and gracious, slow to anger and abounding in steadfast love. He does not deal with us according to our sins, nor requite us according to our iniquities. Psalms 103: 8, 10

Road Sign

When we are not hearing God's voice speaking to our hearts, perhaps we need to turn down the volume on the everyday noise of life.

Still Before You

Lord, when I arise each morning
With the day stretching out before me
Filled with the demands and stress of life,
Remind me to be still before You.

When the pressure mounting throughout the day
Closes in on me, threatening my calm
With its tension and its hurriedness,
Remind me to be still before You.

When life's inevitable and unavoidable sadness
Wraps my soul in its dark clouds
And starts to pull me into its sinking despair,
Remind me to be still before You.

When the never ending and confusing choices
And the ever increasing responsibilities of life
Start to move me in their tailspin,
Remind me to be still before You.

For if I want to hear Your guiding voice
Know Your comforting peace, feel Your tender love
I need to take time often enough and long enough
To be still before You.

For when I am still before You
Long enough, and often enough
That is when I will hear Your guiding voice
Know Your comforting peace, and feel Your tender love.

In quietness and in trust shall be your strength. Isaiah 30:15

Road Sign

Speed bumps and potholes - they slow us down and annoy us. They are easy to tell apart on the road. The difference between them is that one belongs in the road, and the other one doesn't.

Difficulties in life - they can either be speed bumps, placed in our path by God to slow us down when we are in a dangerous area or are about to miss something important. Or they can be potholes, placed in our path by someone who does not want us to reach our destination. In the journey of life, especially when the way grows dark, we sometimes can't tell them apart. The best thing to do when we cannot see what is ahead is to slow down and leave the driving to God. He's capable of driving through any obstacle course!

So Special

You make me feel so special, Lord
Each time You speak to me
Your Spirit reaching out to mine
To whisper tenderly

Of something You would have me do
To help another one
Or saying You forgive me of
The many wrongs I've done.

You make me feel so special, Lord
When you give me a surprise
Like looking out across the sand
I see a pair of eyes

These eyes sit high upon two stalks
On a body small and tan
I laugh at how You made the crab
Walk sideways through the sand!

You make me feel so special, Lord
The times you choose me for
A special job that You want done
Dear Lord, please use me more.

(Continued)

You make me feel so special, Lord
When I feel Your soft caress
Through the gentle, warm spring breeze.
I feel so richly blessed.

You make me feel so special, Lord
When I breathe a worried sigh
Then looking up I see Your love
In a rainbow in the sky.

You make me feel so special, Lord
When You give to me
A very dear and special friend
To keep me company.

You make me feel so special, Lord
As I look up at the stars.
You are so special, He replied,
All of My children are.

The steadfast love of the Lord never ceases, His mercies never come to an end; they are new every morning; great is Thy faithfulness. Lamentations 3:22-23

Roses

In a beautiful garden stands a graceful rosebush, full of lovely, fragrant roses. One day a fierce storm swept through the garden. The winds blew and the rain beat down. Finally, the storm moved on. Although some of the roses were able to withstand the onslaught of the storm, several of the blossoms now hung sadly down, their stems bruised and bent.

Not long after the storm leaves, a man comes walking through the garden. He sees the rosebush and stops to admire the beautiful roses, standing tall and fragrant. He then casts a look of distaste at the drooping roses. He wonders why someone doesn't cut off those drooping roses and, shaking his head, he leaves.

Shortly thereafter, a lady strolls through the garden. She, too, stops to admire the rosebush. She is saddened as she gazes on the drooping roses and reaches out to straighten them. Her fingers close around one of the stems, and are pricked by the thorns. Quickly, she lets the stem drop from her hand and she leaves, nursing her pricked finger.

A third person comes along. When he sees the drooping roses, he too reaches out to straighten them, carefully avoiding the thorns. After straightening a rose, he removes his hand from the stem, and the rose droops forward again. He tries repeatedly, determined to restore this rose to its upright position. But the rose is weak where the stem had been bruised and bent. The repeated, determined efforts of the man finally cause the stem to break and the rose to drop to the ground. The man gives up and leaves.

Finally, the Gardener comes to tend His rosebush. As He approaches, He sees how the storm has damaged His rosebush and how some of the roses are bent and drooping. He sees the one fallen rose, now withering on the ground. He feels sad at the loss of this beautiful flower. Very gently, He reaches out to each bent rose. Tenderly, slowly, He restores each one to its original place on the bush, each flower uplifted towards the sun. As the

Gardener straightens from His task, the sweet fragrance of the restored roses rises up to Him in gratitude. As He turns to leave, He reaches down and picks up the fallen rose. Cradling it lovingly in His arms, He carries it home with Him where He will care for it.

As we go out into the garden of life to help tend to the Gardener's roses, may we handle each one with the same compassion and gentleness that the Gardener Himself has for each rose. If we find any that have fallen, let us carry them to the Gardener's loving arms to be cared for by Him.

With everlasting love I will have compassion on you, says the Lord, your Redeemer. Isaiah 54:8

Into His Eyes

One hot day as the sun beat down
She saw him beside a tree
As she carried her jug to the well
She wondered who he might be.

Watching him, she slowed her step
Hoping to avoid his stare
For people either stared at her
Or pretended she wasn't there.

Quietly, she lowered her jug
To the water far below
Hoping he wouldn't notice her
And quickly she could go.

She was startled when he spoke
Closing her eyes with dread
He asked her for some water to drink
And slowly she lifted her head.

"What do you really want from me?"
She asked with great distrust
The men she knows either put her down
Or see her with eyes of lust.

"Bring your husband here" he asked.
Her face creased in a frown.
"I have no husband" she replied
As she looked down at the ground.

(Continued)

"You have had five" this man then said
And she looked up with surprise
"And the man you're with won't marry you."
She stared into his eyes.

Expecting to see contempt and hate
And judgment, harsh but true
To hear words of cruel insult
with condemnation too.

But she saw eyes of compassion
His heart was filled with love
He extended to her forgiveness
From His Father up above.

For Jesus cared much more about
The person deep inside
Than He was the wrongful things
That she wished to hide.

As you approach life's empty well
You'll see the Waiting One
His heart full of forgiving love
No matter what you've done.

If you'll just look into His eyes
As this woman dared to do
You'll find no condemnation there
Just His great love for you.

With joy you will draw water from the wells of salvation.
Isaiah 12:3

The Present

There was a man who had a wonderful present. It was the most wonderful present anyone could ever hope to have. He wanted nothing more than to find someone he could give this present to.

First, the man went to a friend and offered him the present. The friend looked at the present and then looked at the man with a cautious look. "Why do you want to give me this present" the friend asked. "Because you are my friend and I care about you." the man softly answered. "None of my friends have ever offered me such a present without wanting something in return. I don't want to be indebted to anyone!" the friend stated firmly. The man left, feeling sad that his friend did not understand that there were no strings attached to his present.

Next, he went to a young lady he knew and showed the present to her. "What a wonderful present this is! Nothing could be better than this!" she exclaimed. The man was so happy as he asked her "Then you will accept my present, won't you?" "Oh, no," she replied. "I'm just a plain, poor girl. There's no way that I could accept such a wonderful present. I certainly don't deserve it." Then she walked away. The man knew that no one would ever deserve this present, but it was one he wanted to give them anyway.

He took his present to a neighbor. His neighbor told him, "That's certainly a fine present. Wouldn't mind having that myself." "Then it's yours," the man cheerfully said. But the neighbor refused saying, "I couldn't accept it until I clean up around here and remodel this old house. That present is too nice to have it in here the way things are." The man tried to convince the neighbor that all that work would not be necessary in order to accept the present, but the neighbor wouldn't hear of it.

Soon after, the man offered the present to a young man he met. The young man was very impressed with the present and it was obvious that he really wanted it. "How much will you take for it?" he asked. The man was surprised that anyone would offer him money for his present. He told the young man, "This present is not for sale." The young man replied, "There's no way I could accept something like that without paying for it first." The man again told him, "This present is not for sale. If I sold it, it would then just be merchandise, and not a present." The young man remarked, "It's a shame you won't let me buy it. I sure would have liked having it," and he went on his way.

Continuing his search for someone to give his present to, the man came upon a woman with several children. She looked so tired and lonely. It appeared that she did not have much and was working hard to provide for her little ones. He thought she surely would want his present. She looked at the present with a longing in her eyes, and then told the man, "As much as I would like the present, I can't afford it. But perhaps I could do some work for you. I can clean a house until it shines and I bake the most mouth-watering apple pie you ever tasted!" "No, no," the man sadly answered, "this is a present. It's not wages that can be earned." The woman told him, "Well, I don't have much, but I do have my pride. I won't be taking hand outs!" So he sadly left the woman with her children and her pride.

The man then went into a grocery store and there he ran into a friend he had not seen for a long time. They exchanged hellos and the friend told the man that he was picking up some groceries and medicine for his sick children. The man showed his friend the present. The friend told the man, "This is such a wonderful present. I feel honored that you have offered it to me. Yes, I'll be glad to accept it. Just let me get these groceries and this medicine home to my children and I'll come by and get it later." The man tried to get him to take the present with him, but the friend insisted on coming back to get it later. Several days passed, and the friend called the man to tell him that he still wanted the present, but he was so busy working overtime now. He would have to wait until he got his work caught up to pick up the present from the man. A considerable amount of time went by and the man had not heard from his friend. Finally, he called his friend's house and the friend's wife answered the phone. "Yes, my husband told me about the present. I'm very sorry to have to tell you this, but my husband became very ill with what the children had. Although they all got better, he didn't and he died yesterday. It's a shame he never got by to get the present from you. He thought he had plenty of time to accept it, but tragically, he didn't. I know he really wanted to have it, but it's too late now."

The man felt so sad. He has such a wonderful present, but he can't find anyone to give it to. It doesn't cost anything. You don't have to do anything to earn it. Anyone can have it, no matter who he is or what he does in life. Wait, what about you? Would you be interested? Come closer and I'll show it to you. Here, look. Isn't that the most wonderful present you could ever want? All you have to do is accept it. Just say, "Yes I want it. I may not deserve it. I can't afford it. I don't want to wait either. I want to accept it right now."

You see, the man with the present is really the Lord Jesus Christ. The present He is offering is His forgiveness and His gift of eternal life. None of us deserve it. Its cost is more than we could ever afford. But He already bought it and there's nothing He wants more than to have you accept it. Will you? Don't put it off until a better day, because there's no such thing. If you're wondering why He would offer you a present like this, it's for the same reason you give presents to your children. Simply because He loves you. As far as He's concerned, that's reason enough.

Thanks be to God for His inexpressible gift! 2 Corinthians 9:15

He Seeks Us in So Many Ways

He seeks us in so many ways
Though we may not be aware
All around He's showing us
How much He really cares.

Nature tells us silently
In mountains standing tall
That God is still the ruler of
All things both great and small.

The drops of water falling down
From rain clouds up above
Bring with them the hope of life
Like God's life-giving love.

The rainbow sends its colors forth
God's promise to declare
His love is everlasting
Eternal is His care.

White and fluffy clouds drift by
As if searching from above
The ones who are the object of
God's mercy and His love.

As you listen to a dove
Sing his "Coo, coo, coo"
You can almost hear His voice
Saying "I love you".

As a mighty gust of wind
Bends the tree limb low
His hand of love is reaching down
To each of us below.

The flowing river ever seeks
The ocean far away
Symbolic of the way that God
Seeks us every day.

Stars wink at us as if to say
A secret we'll tell you
God's seeking you both day and night
In everything you do.

The fragrance lingers from the rain
The air feels fresh and new
Much like the life that God desires
To give to me and you.

He seeks us in so many ways
And waits so patiently
For us to hear Him as He speaks
His love to truly see.

The heavens are telling the glory of God; and the firmament proclaims His handiwork. Psalms 19:1

Road Sign

Would you rather have all that you want or all that He is willing to give?

Would you be willing to give away all that you hold on to in order to receive everything He wants you to give you?

The Shell and the Sand Dollar

One day as I walked slowly down
A beach with sand so white
The waves were rushing to the shore
The sun was shining bright.

Not many people were around
I walked on silently
With so much weighing on my mind
As I gazed out at the sea.

Lifting my eyes heavenward
I then poured out my heart
To a good and loving God
And asked for a new start.

I wanted to give action to
The words I easily speak
I felt the time for me had come
The will of God to seek.

As I left the beach that day
I carried in my hand
A pair of shells joined at their side
A symbol of His plan.

(Continued)

In order to be used by God
We must be like those shells
Whole and lying open
Emptied of ourselves.

The next day as I walked again
Down beside the sea
Somehow I felt that I would find
Something there for me.

My heart was filled with wonder when
I spotted in the sand
The form of a sand dollar
And I took it in my hand.

I gazed upon this object
God washed up from the sea
And thought about its legend
How it tells of Calvary.

My heart was overflowing
With the fullness of His love
I've never felt such closeness to
My Father up above.

For one day God provided
Two shells to help me see
That the first step I must take
Is to be open and empty.

The next day God completed
A picture that's so real
He provides the Holy Spirit
Our emptiness to fill.

Now when I go walking
Down beside the sea
I pause to thank Him for the love
He gives us tenderly.

And I think about the lesson
He taught so beautifully
With a shell and a sand dollar
He washed up from the sea.

Create in me a clean heart, O God, and put a new and right spirit within me. Psalms 51:10

Road Sign

It's impossible for us to complain about life and laugh with joy - both at the same moment.
God's Word tells us to praise Him even in the midst of trouble.

Is this His cure for the complaining Christian?

You Can Praise

How do you praise when you're hurting
How do you get past the pain
When all you really want to feel
Is health and strength again?

How do you praise when you're crying
Don't the tears just get in the way?
It would be easier to gladly rejoice
On a brighter, happier day.

How do you praise when you're lonely
And you think that nobody cares?
How do you find praise in your heart
When your soul feels painfully bare?

How do you praise when you're failing
And everything seems to go wrong?
It seems almost impossible
To find even one praise song.

(Continued)

You can praise even when you are hurting
For you do not suffer alone
If His eye is on the sparrow
He will certainly care for His own.

You can still praise when you are crying
For God understands your despair
He's the one who wipes away tears
With His tender loving care.

You can praise God when you are lonely
For He knows what you are going through
For when His Son hung on the cross
He experienced loneliness too.

You can praise God when you are failing
And you cannot find a song to sing
Because of the death of Christ on a cross
God can forgive us of anything.

Because Thy steadfast love is better than life, my lips shall praise Thee. Psalms 63:3

Reflections

I now have plenty time each day
To reflect on days gone by
To think back how it used to be
How the time did fly.

Remembering when I was a child
That seems so long ago
Running carefree through the grass
I couldn't wait to grow.

Life was so much different then
Than it is today
Times were hard and we were poor
But Lord You showed the way.

Daddy worked so very hard
Through days both hot and long
Mama made our house a home
Because her faith was strong.

Though we didn't have the things
We can't live without today
We had something better still
We knew how to laugh and play.

For life went at a slower pace
When there was time to talk
About anything and nothing much
On a cool spring evening walk.

(Continued)

Now my life has changed so much
I sit alone each day
My family doesn't have the time
For hearing words I long to say.

I could tell them all about
The way life used to be
And share some of the wisdom
That God has given me.

For I have seen so many things
Throughout my many years
Depression, war, prosperity
I've known both hope and fear.

Young folk think that I don't know
About the world today
But I know what they sometimes forget
God does not change His ways.

The world has changed so very much
And yet it stays the same
Man still walks in darkness
When God's love he will not claim.

As I sit with my reflections
Remind me, Lord, each day
That there is more that I can do
To help to light the way.

Although I can no longer read
With eyes that have grown dim
Through the vision of my soul
I can still see Him.

My voice is not so very strong
For telling of His love
But I can lift my heart in prayer
To my Father up above.

When I think about my family
Although I miss them so
I know my prayers will be with them
No matter where they go.

My hands and feet can't take me
To lands across the sea
I can still reach out in love
To the one sitting by me.

Though I have reflections
Of the years that I have lived
Help me reflect on You, my Lord
And the love I still can give.

Do not cast me off in the time of old age; forsake me not when my strength is spent. Psalms 71:9

DEATH

A Journey Ends

From this side, death appears to be the end of our journey. From God's side, it can be the beginning of a wonderful new life or of an eternity of hell - it's our choice.

Ending Before Beginning

A life's journey deliberately ended before it can even begin. What could break God's heart more, and yet, still be forgiven by Him?

A Chance to Live

Imagine that you were born at a time far into the future. Science has advanced greatly in the study of genetics. Before a child is even conceived, they can test both parents and determine the future the child they are considering bringing into this world will have. The government has made the testing mandatory, but the final decision of whether or not to conceive this child still remains with the potential parents. Reluctantly, you have the test taken, and you sit in the doctor's office, awaiting the results.

The words you hear come as a blow. The recommendation is not to conceive. You brace yourself for the reason, wondering if it will be a physical defect, a mental or emotional deficiency, or something even worse. The physical defect you could handle. Even a mental or emotional deficiency could be coped with. But what is laid out before you is the worse scenario you could face.

This child, not yet conceived, would grow to be become one of the worst criminals of your day. What hardships would be placed on you and your family? What pain would be inflicted on society? What kind of life is that to expect your child to have to live? How do you make that kind of decision? Are you able and willing to pay the price that this child will cost you, in so many ways? If there is even the smallest chance that this child could, at some point in his life, be set free from this horrible life of crime, would it be worth the risk, knowing the greater chance of failure?

I wonder, did God ask Himself these same questions before He created each of us?

Surely, knowing all things He knew we would fall into the type of life that would separate us from Him. Even if he provided a way of setting us free from it, He must have known that not all of us would accept this freedom. How great His love for us must have been, even before He created us, even before He said "Let there be light". He still chose to create us, although He knew that the way we would live would demand a cost that would be paid by many, including and especially His own Son.

That Christ would die for us is too amazing to comprehend. That God would even bother to create us to begin with, knowing the things we would do, amazes me even more. He didn't have to create us. He didn't need us. He was God and He was complete in Himself, without us. The answer can only be found in His love, and yet this answer is beyond anything we could ever understand. He loved us enough to give us a chance to live, no matter what the possible outcome and no matter the cost to Him. Would we have done the same? Thank God that His ways are not our ways, for it they were, none of us might be here today.

The Lord God formed man of dust from the ground, and breathed into his nostrils the breath of life; and man became a living being. Genesis 2:7

A New Life

Darkness surrounds me. I float contentedly. My little heart has been beating for a while now. I wonder what the future holds for me. I haven't yet figured out if I'm a boy or a girl. I wonder what kind of parents I'll have. Will my mom rock me while she sings a lullaby? Will my daddy play with me and bounce me on his knee? Will I have any brothers or sisters?

Looks like we're at the doctor's office again. We've been here a few times before. I wonder if he'll poke at me again?

What is that thing in here with me? It's too dark to see it and my eyes aren't finish forming yet. Something's wrong. What's happening? Why do I feel like something's burning me? Mommy! Don't you want me? I'm your child. I need you. My body is being pulled apart! No!! I can't stand it! Mommy! Mommy! Mommm........

Before I formed you in the womb, I knew you, and before you were born I consecrated you. Jeremiah 1:5

Encounter With A Stranger

She left her desk and walked down the empty hallway to get herself a cup of water. But to her dismay, she found the hallway wasn't empty at all. A stranger stood near the water fountain. An odd feeling that something was about to happen came over her. She shook off the thought of returning to her office. She was safe. Other employees worked right behind the closed doors lining the hallway.

As she reached above the water fountain for a paper cup, the stranger asked her if she would also get him a cup of water. "Excuse me, sir," she said, "I don't mean to be rude, but I don't see why you can't get your own cup of water." She was in no mood to flirt with any man today, let alone one who couldn't even come up with a decent "pick up line". The stranger spoke softly saying, "I didn't mean to offend you. It was just my way of starting a conversation. What I'd really like is to see your baby." What a strange request to make, especially in an office and especially of her. "I don't have a baby," she replied, hoping that would be the end of an unwanted conversation. But something in the man's eyes held hers in a knowing gaze. "You're right" he said "for you've had five abortions and you don't plan to continue with this pregnancy" as his eyes briefly lowered to her still flat abdomen, then raised up to catch her shocked gaze.

Instinctively, her hand moved across her stomach. "How could you know," she asked "since I just found out this morning myself, at home? No one else knows!" "My child," he answered, "I know more than that. I know how to give you back your life, to provide hope for this baby, and to give life back to your other five babies." He spoke words that were hard to believe, but with a voice that left no room for disbelief. "But how? I've messed up my life beyond salvaging. I have nothing to offer this baby. And the others are already . . ." her voice trailed off as her throat began to tighten and a glistening tear formed in her eyes.

He spoke to her with such understanding and compassion. "I created your life, and I can recreate it anew. I can give you the strength you'll need to provide a loving home for this new life you now carry, and I've already given your other babies new lives, with my own dear Father to be their parents. He wants to be your Heavenly Father too, if you'll only let Him." Incredulously, she said, "But after all I've done . . ." He cut her off saying, "My Father and I don't approve of what you've done. Instead of taking responsibility for the lives you helped to conceive, you tried to escape the problems that went with the responsibility by denying the sanctity of life. But We've never stopped loving you or being concerned about the difficulties you've been going through, and We never will. We are here to forgive the past, and to help you with the rest of your life. One day, We'd like to take you to Our home, where you'll be able to hold all your children again."

He extended His hand of love and hope to her. She stood still for a moment, pondering all He had said to her. Then slowly, hesitantly she placed her small, trembling hand into His, and with it her troubled life and the life of her unborn baby.

Eight months later, as she stood in the same hallway getting another cup of water, she felt the beginnings of her first contraction, and she breathed a silent thank-you to the Stranger by the water fountain. Except now, He was no longer a stranger in her heart.

I have set before you life and death, blessing and curse; therefore choose life, that you and your descendants may live, loving the Lord your God, obeying His voice, and cleaving to Him, for that means life to you. Deuteronomy 30:19-20

A Journey Completed

The journey is all we know. The journey is part of who we are. For the journey to end feels like we will end too. But God has shared His surprise with us. The end of the journey is only the beginning.

The Beginning of a New Life

God sends forth His love, and a new life begins. Day by day, I grow more and more. At first, I don't even know I exist. But my heart is there. As I grow, I slowly become aware of the environment I am in. Each day, I discover something new. I sleep. I awake. I move. As I grow, I sometimes bump into my environment. It holds me. This is my world. Outside of it is someone who loves me, but I am oblivious to it. At times, I feel a gentle prodding from outside my little world. I move away from that touch. As my sense of hearing is developing, I often hear a voice faintly, but I don't understand it. Sometimes, I think I hear singing and music from outside my world. Occasionally, my world moves. I enjoy the gentle sway. Sometimes, the sudden moves startle me. My sight begins to form, but things are dim in my world. Overall, I like it here. But as I grow, I'm starting to feel uncomfortable. I seem to be outgrowing this place.

Then, one day, something starts to happen. I'm not sure I like this. I'm being pushed from my world. No, I don't want to leave it! It's been home for me. Perhaps I am getting uncomfortable there, but I really don't mind. Please let me stay! I'm afraid of the prodding, the voices, and sometimes of even the singing that's been outside my world. Won't someone listen to me?!

What's this? This isn't like the world I've been growing in. It was dark in there. Look at the light and the different colors. I'm being wrapped in something soft and warm. There's that singing again, but it's no longer distant and muffled. It's beautiful. And there are strong arms holding me. I feel so safe. This is wonderful. Why was I so afraid? Why did I ever think that being placed in my Heavenly Father's arms was death?

Even though I walk through the valley of the shadow of death, I fear no evil. Psalms 23:4

There's So Much More

There is so much more for me to do
Chores in the house and outside too
How I enjoy taking care of my place
It really puts a smile on my face.

But I can no longer cut the grass
I've not even the strength to take out the trash
For sickness now fills my body with pain
I'll never do all those things again.

I have a family whom I love so
I don't want to be a burden, you know
But I'm not even able to take care of me
Let alone look after my dear family.

I'm really not an elderly man
If so, I might could understand
There's still more life I want to live
There's still more love I want to give.

Then the Lord spoke to my heart
"This isn't the end, just a new start
True life is not measured by time alone
You are My child, your life will go on.

Real life began when you trusted in Me
And will continue for eternity
The only difference is where you will live
Your love you will continue to give.

For your love lives on in your children and wife
And each one you've touched in this earthly life
In Heaven, there's so much more to do
Just wait till you see what I've planned for you!

A place to live made with you in mind
Surrounded by flowers, your favorite kind
You can walk among them and not tire out
You can run or dance, sing or shout.

Don't worry about the last trip you'll make
For when the time comes, your hand I will take
I will lead you home to Heaven above
The way will be bright with the light of My love.

I'll personally show you around the place
And welcome you there with a loving embrace
Then one day I'll tell you to come and wait
For someone to join you at the Eastern Gate.

What a special homecoming that will be
When you see your wife enter Heaven with me
Both reunited with family and friends
You'll never have to leave them again.

So in the days that still remain
When you must suffer with this life's pain
Remember the best is yet to be
When we are together in eternity."

Blessed be the God and Father of our Lord Jesus Christ! By His great mercy we have been born anew to a living hope through the resurrection of Jesus Christ from the dead and to an inheritance which is imperishable, undefiled, and unfading, kept in heaven for you. 1 Peter 1:3-4

In Your Hands

Dear Lord, we place the precious life
Of a loved one in Your hands
We do not know just how to pray
We do not know Your plans.

Our hearts are hurting as we watch
His suffering and his pain
Should we ask You to take him
Or let him here remain?

Lord, we know that You are love
And You see more than we do
Therefore in peace we can turn
His life over to You.

Whatever happens on this day
We know it's for the best
If you give him health and life
Or provide his final rest.

We only ask of You, dear Lord
Whatever is Your plan
That You will stay close by his side
Held in Your loving hands.

Give us peace deep in our hearts
Surrendering all to You
Sometimes that is the hardest thing
That You ask us to do.

And when the day is over
Whatever the outcome be
Let us thank you for Your matchless love
And give our praise to Thee.

Looking to Jesus the pioneer and perfector of our faith. Hebrews 12:2

Last Goodbye

It's not easy for me to say goodbye
Not after all these years
Somehow I just can't say the word
It gets lost in all the tears.

You were there for me back when
My first small step I took
Steadying the bike I learned to ride
Reading me my first book.

There were times when we were close
I'll treasure those times always
And there were times when we argued
Those times now haunt my days.

But, Dad, now that you have gone
Home to Heaven up above
I know you now can understand
And forgive with perfect love.

There are regrets within my heart
Of a closeness that might have been
But I know one day it will be that way
When in Heaven I see you again.

Dad, the time has sadly come
To say our last goodbye
I told myself that I'd be strong
I did not want to cry.

Although I know you're in a place
Where from suffering you're set free
An empty place within my life
Right now is all I see.

But memories of our good times
Will fill that empty space
I'll live my life to make you proud
When again I see your face.

Dad, before I leave you now
One more thing I want to do
To thank you for all you did for me
And tell you I love you.

Hearken to your father who begat you. Proverbs 23:22

My Husband

He is gone, I can't believe it
He was the best part of my life
He was my partner and my lover
I was proud to be his wife.

I wake up in the morning
Alone in our soft bed
I look upon the pillow
Where he used to lay his head.

There is no smell of his cologne
No clothes upon the floor
Oh how happy I would be
To pick up his things once more.

I long to hear his gentle voice
To hear his "I love you"
Peacefully to rest within
His arms the whole night through.

Those days are gone forever
How quickly they did past
I never truly realized
It would go by quite that fast.

My days are all so long now
Lonely ones that never end
There's no one to share my days with
For I've lost my dearest friend.

Dear God, why did You take him?
He was everything to me.
How am I to go on now
Without his company?

He didn't want to leave me
Nor I to let him go
But you took him on to Heaven
And left me here below.

I think about him walking
Along the streets of gold
Once again united
With family and friends of old.

One day I know I'll see him
When I depart his place
Then I will see the smile I miss
When again I see his face.

Although I may be lonely
And miss him every night
My memories of him will help
To make each dark dawn bright.

Although he's gone, I thank you Lord
For the best part of my life
He was my partner and my lover
I was proud to be his wife.

The Lord is near to the brokenhearted, and saves the crushed in spirit. Psalms 34:18

My Wife

She is gone, I can't believe it
She was the best part of my life
She was my partner and my confidante
My lover and my wife.

I wake up in the morning
Alone in our soft bed
I look upon the pillow
Where she used to lay her head.

There's no smell of breakfast cooking
Of coffee rich and strong
No sound of her in the kitchen
Humming a happy song.

My days are all so long now
Lonely ones that never end
There's no one to share my days with
For I've lost my dearest friend.

Dear God, why did You take her?
She was everything to me.
How am I to live my life now
Without her company?

But deep within my heart I know
That she's with You above
She didn't leave with heavy heart
But on the wings of love.

She didn't want to leave me
Nor I to let her go
But you took her on to Heaven
And left me here below.

I think about her walking
Along the streets of gold
Once again united
With family and friends of old.

Once again I'll see her
When I depart his place
Then I will see the smile I miss
When again I see her face.

Although I may be lonely
And miss her every night
My memories of her will help
To make each dark dawn bright.

Although she's gone, I thank you Lord
For the best part of my life
She was my partner and my confidante
My lover and my wife.

The Lord is near to the brokenhearted, and saves the crushed in spirit. Psalms 34:18

Road Sign

Have you ever expected a child to accept your "no" without explanation because the explanation was too difficult for the child to understand, or it wasn't the right time for an explanation?

Sometimes it's difficult for us to trust God to be wise enough not to answer all of our questions the way we want them answered, and without always giving us an explanation.

Why?

Why did you take him away from me
Just when I needed him so?
I needed my dad to be with me
To help me learn and grow.

I was so very young that day
I could not understand
Why you took my dad away
Was that part of Your plan?

Lord, did it make you happy when
You saw this small boy cry?
No one had the answer to
"Why did my daddy die?"

Although the tears all soon were gone
Life never was the same
I could not have my daddy there
To watch my first ball game.

No throwing baseballs back and forth
No father and son talks
Without my dad my life would be
A lonely path to walk.

It hurt so much when I would see
Other boys beside their dads
Why did You have to take from me
The only dad I had?

(Continued)

Now that I've become a man
With a son to call my own
I think about my father still
And I feel so all alone.

How can I forgive you Lord
For causing me such pain?
I don't think I will ever want
To talk with You again.

My anger runs so deep inside
I cannot let it go
You have really hurt me Lord
More than You'll ever know.

"My child," the Lord said tenderly,
"I know you're hurting so
Any where away from Me
Is where you want to go.

You think that I'm the one to blame
For all that you've been through
As if I did it just to cause
All this pain for you.

Right now you cannot understand
All the things I do
It may be hard for you to know
I really do love you.

I never promised anyone
That life would have no pain
But you have My own assurance that
You'll see your dad again.

On that day you'll understand
The things you now can't see
You can trust My every move
Because of Calvary.

I would never send My Son
To die upon a cross
Then just turn My back on you
While you suffer such a loss.

When life holds trials and sufferings
That make no sense to man
That's when I'm willing to draw close
And hold you in My hand.

I may not always take away
The things you must go through
But if you'll only let Me in
I'll always be with you."

We know that as you share in our sufferings, you will also share in our comfort. 2 Corinthians 1:7

HEAVEN OR HELL
After the Journey

Some people get so caught up with the journey of life, that they never decide where the journey will be taking them. Others think they can decide where they are going once they arrive there (their thinking is as mixed up as that sounds). Some people think that the journey is all there is. Unfortunately, the only way to reach the destination of your choice is to make sure you are on the right journey. Do you know where your journey is taking you? Jesus said, "I am the Way".

Heaven

The destination of choice.

The place where all God-led journeys end.

Don't miss the welcome home party planned for you. It's "out of this world".

Road Sign

You've been traveling for a long time. You've seen a lot of scenery and had some wonderful adventures. You met many other interesting travelers and even helped some along their journey. You also had your own share of breakdowns and flat tires along the way. Although you've been feeling tired and sleepy during this last stretch, seeing your destination come into view perks you up and you know that you will be able to finish the trip.

Won't it be nice to finally be home? Isn't it nice to know that Someone will be waiting up for you?

The Contents of Heaven

What won't be in Heaven:

Broken hearts
Funerals
Illness
Boredom
Sadness
Loneliness
Anger
Hatred
Good-byes
_____ (fill in whatever makes you unhappy)

What will be in Heaven:

Laughter
Fun
Excitement
Contentment
Companionship
Quiet peacefulness
Exuberant celebration
Jesus
Me
You (I hope!)
_____ (fill in whatever makes you happy)

What makes one person happy is often different than what makes someone else happy. Even the same person will find happiness in varying things throughout the changing seasons of life.

We do not know exactly what Heaven will be like. We can rest assured in this - God will provide whatever He knows we will need to make it, well, "Heavenly" for each and everyone of us who has made that our final destination.

It seems natural for us to fear the unknown, and Heaven can seem like an "unknown" for us. God has not chosen to reveal all the details about Heaven to us. Perhaps it would make it too difficult for us to continue with our lives now if we knew all that awaited us. Perhaps God wants us to learn to trust Him. Perhaps God is looking forward to our look of delighted surprise when He reveals that gift to us! Whatever the reason that He has kept the details of Heaven a secret, we have no need to fear this wonderful gift, for we already know the Giver, and He is kind and good, and He loves us.

What no eye has seen, nor ear heard, nor the heart of man conceived, what God has prepared for those who love Him. 1 Corinthians 2:9

Road Sign

We often wish that God would intervene and make everything right. Before destroying all the wrong things and taking away all hope for the lost, perhaps God is waiting for someone you love to make things right with Him.

If a holy, just God, who feels all our pains, can be patient with this world's sin and suffering in order to reach one more person for eternity, can't we undeserving yet forgiven sinners endure just a little longer too? Our sufferings are only for a short while on this earth. The suffering of a lost one is for eternity without end.

Tears in Heaven

Imagine that the time has come
When you stand in Heaven above
The time of judgment has arrived
But you're protected by His love.

For long ago you made the choice
To ask Him in your heart
Now you know that you are His
From Him you'll never depart.

But as you stand there uncondemned
What of those whom you loved so
The ones who do not know the Lord
The ones who told Him "no".

A sad time it will be for all
Even if you know the Lord
For you will watch the rejection of
Those who rejected His Word.

Then they all will understand
They should have accepted Him
But now their chance has come and gone
There is no hope for them.

(Continued)

How our hearts will surely break
Seeing loved ones sent away
To remember all the times that we
Could have warned them of this day.

We'll look back at all the things
We thought we had to do
Too busy to tell a dear lost one
About God's love so true.

Too afraid to take a stand
Afraid of what they'd say
Words that might have saved them from
The pain of judgment day.

When at last it all is done
Then God will turn to you
He knows just what you're feeling
For His heart is broken too.

He'll reach out to wipe away
The tears upon your face
Once again He'll show to us
His unchanging grace.

And though we all will have our tears
How much better it would be
The rejection of the ones we love
We'd never have to see.

Let's ask God to give us strength
And the words we need to say
To reach our loved ones for the Lord
That they might not turn away.

Imagine that the day has come
When you stand in Heaven above
And sharing in your tears of joy
Are all the ones you love.

He will wipe away every tear from their eyes, and death shall be no more, neither shall there be mourning nor crying nor pain any more. Revelation 21:4

Left Alone

Oh Lord, I'm deeply troubled for
I heard somebody say
That the time is coming when
You'll take Your hand away.

Those living here will have to face
A life unlike we've known
Where death and pain is everywhere
Where Satan rules his own.

There will be so many who
Have good and caring hearts
They will not understand it when
The tribulation starts.

People think the world is bad
With all its hate and crime
But it's nothing like what is to come
In that God forsaken time.

They will cry out for Your help
But it will be in vain
No longer will you lend Your ear
To listen to their pain.

There won't be any angels sent
By Your own caring hand
To stop the growing panic
That will spread across the land.

Miracles will cease to be
And men will realize
Just how much they didn't see
With unbelieving eyes.

There will be an emptiness
That's not been felt before
The Spirit of a living God
Exists on earth no more.

These days of fear and such unrest
I know I'll never see
For You'll make sure that I am safe
In Heaven I will be.

Because there was a blessed day
Your loving voice I heard
When I asked Jesus in my heart
As Savior and as Lord.

(Continued)

But what about the ones I love
Who will be left behind
I won't be there to tell them of
A Savior's love so kind.

It breaks my heart to think about
The things they will go through
And that's just the beginning
For hell awaits them too.

Oh Lord, please help me care enough
To do what I can do
No matter what the cost might be
To tell them about You.

Then I'll know that on the day
You come to claim Your own
They will hear their name called too.
They'll not be left alone.

And convince some, who doubt; save some, by snatching them out of the fire. Jude 1:22-23

Hell

A destination to be avoided at all costs.

The cost was set - death on a cross for us.
The cost was paid - death on a cross by Him.

WARNING!!!!

The following writing will not give you the warm fuzzies.

Read at your own risk.

CAUTION!!!

The Eternity of Hell

Unquenchable thirst. I long for a drop of water, but it doesn't come. I beg. I plead. No one hears me. There is no cool water to be had. My soul is on fire, but the well of God's love is no longer available for me.

Unending loneliness. Others are around me, but they are ever consumed with their own suffering. They cannot relieve me of mine. Never again will I know compassion, friendship, love.

Unfading memories. I cannot escape the thoughts of loved ones I will never see again. I know now that they exist in another place beyond the confines of my eternal prison. My heart breaks constantly.

Unrelinquishing pain. All the hurts and heartaches of my earthly life continuously haunt me. There is no escaping the pain. My regrets act as salt in my open wounds.

Unparalleled suffering. Not even the greatest hurt of my earthly life can compare to this. At least, in that life you knew the suffering would eventually end, even if it was in death. Although death ended earth's temporal suffering, for me it only led to a greater suffering.

Unspeakable torment. Of all the suffering I must continue to endure, the worst part is being totally cut off from God. In my life, I didn't believe He existed. Now, it feels like He has stopped believing that I exist. I never realized how much I needed Him until it was too late.

Unnumbered days. The days here have no beginning or end. There is no need to number them. It would make no difference. At first, you long for relief. But relief does not exist here. It's difficult to imagine no end to it - no hope. But as eternity passes, realization and understanding sets in. Eternity continues like a circle. My eternity is a circle of misery and despair.

Undeniable truth. The hardest part of being here is knowing that I didn't have to come here. God tried so hard through family, friends, and even strangers to get me to accept His love and forgiveness. But I was too proud; too stubborn. I thought I knew better. Now, all that's left for me is the eternity of hell.

What's left for you?

If any one's name was not found written in the book of life, he was thrown into the lake of fire. Revelation 20:15

SPECIAL DAYS

God-Given Rest Stops for the Journey

God knows that we often get so caught up with surviving the journey that we lose sight of our destination. When that happens, we can become tired and discouraged. So, He planned rest stops for us to help remind us what the journey is all about.

Lord's Supper

Did you know that at one time your journey came to a dead end? Satan had placed an obstacle so high, so deep, and so wide right at the end so that there would be no way you could ever get past it. But Jesus broke through that obstacle, and paved the way for each of us to reach our destination. The only thing strong enough to break through that obstacle of sin was His own holy body, His own holy life.

This is My Body

These are My feet.
Young feet that played and ran in front of a carpenter's house.
Experienced feet that walked the hot, dusty roads of Jerusalem.
Tired feet, washed with a woman's tears and lovingly dried with her hair.
Bruised feet, impaled with crude Roman nails as the hammer repeatedly fell, driving the stakes through them to the plank that laid beneath Me.

These are My hands.
Gentle hands that reached out to bless the innocent children.
Strong hands with the power to heal the sick and restore life to the dying, and to give peace to guilty hearts.
A Son's hands that extended upward in prayer to My Father.
Holy hands, torn, bleeding, throbbing, with no relief as they strained against the spikes holding them to a beam of rough wood.

This is My body.
An infant's body, caressed by Mary's hands, wrapped in swaddling clothes, and laid in a manger.
A man's body, that felt the sun's warmth, the wind's touch, but also all the pains and desires of any other man, yet remaining pure and holy.
A human body, facing an avoidable death, exhausted from the struggle between fear and obedience, and covered with sweat as I agonized over what lay ahead of Me.
A Savior's body, rent and bruised, tortured just short of death itself, and kept on a cross, not by the iron stakes forced into My hands and feet, but by the love in My heart, until justice for mankind was satisfied through My suffering.

"And He took bread, and gave thanks, and brake it, and gave unto them, saying, 'This is My body which is given for you; this do in remembrance of Me.'"

This is My blood.

Righteous blood which, from the thorns pressed into My head, trickled down My face, into My eyes, onto My lips, not unlike the tears that had once trickled down My face for the hurting and the lost.

Sinless blood that dropped repeatedly from My hands to form darkening pools on the parched ground as it formed pools of relief for parched souls.

Holy blood which slowly ran from My feet, causing stains on the splintered tree on which I hung, washing stains from the hearts of men for whom I died.

My precious blood that poured freely from My side, intertwining with mercy, hope, and grace, flowing with new life and with God's tender love for you.

"And He took the cup, and gave thanks, and gave it to them, saying, 'Drink ye all of it; for this is My blood of the new testament, which was shed for many for the remission sins.'"

This is My love.

Scripture verses taken from the King James Version.

Easter

Easter brings springtime to our journey. It also brings the promise of an everlasting springtime, where life will be ever new and wonderful in His spring garden.

Upon That Cross

As nails were driven
The cross was raised
Silent angels waited
For this was the day
When the love of God for all mankind was lifted upon a cross
To offer forgiveness and grace to a world wandering and lost
Within the darkness and the damp cold of the tomb He did lay
To bring to us life and hope when He rose upon the third day
Our sin was forgiven
Our eternity secured
When all we deserved
He willingly endured
Sacrificing His life
Upon this cruel tree
To reach out in love
To redeem you and me
Do you know His love
Your sin washed away
Look upon that cross
It shows you the way

If we confess our sins, He is faithful and just, and will forgive our sins and cleanse us from all unrighteousness. 1 John 1:9

Thoughts on Easter

Jesus

Did Jesus always know He would be going to the cross? Lying in a manger, did He know? A small child in the temple, did He know? As He lived on this earth, each day bringing Him closer to His destiny, did He often think of what lay ahead? Did a certain hill in the distance loom as an ever present reminder of His ultimate destination?

The Cross

As Jesus hung on the cross, death slowly and relentlessly tightening its grip, what was going through His mind? Did He long for it finally to be over, when death's grip would once and for all be broken? As the thief mocked Him, telling Him to save them as well as Himself, did He think of how easy it would be to do just that? Did Satan whisper lies in His ear, trying to entice Him to come down from the cross? The thieves had no choice. They were kept on their crosses by nails in their hands and feet. But this pure, holy, all-powerful Son of God! No nails on this earth could ever hold Him. Yet, there He stayed. Through the heat of the day. Through the physical torture. Through the jeers and taunts. Through the tears in His mother's eyes. Through the weight of sin. Through the abandonment of His Father in Heaven. Even through death itself. Jesus was kept on His cross by just one thing - the love in His heart for us.

Angels

Angels, who once sang joyfully over Bethlehem, proclaiming a baby's birth, now silent. Angels, allowed to watch, but not to intervene.

God

This was *His* Son who was suffering. The Son who was with Him during creation. The Son who once laid cradled in Mary's arms. The Son who, only yesterday, said "Not My will, but Thine, Father." He watched as Jesus was humiliated. He watched as Jesus was tortured. Finally, the time came when He would have to turn away and allow His Son to face death alone.

Satan

Was Satan naive enough to think that he was at last victorious? Did he mock the now silent angels that had refused to join him long ago? Did he laugh in God's face as Jesus finally died?

It's finished.

It is finished. What next? Did life in the city go on as usual? Or did people whisper about the strange events that happened on that Friday, casting glances toward an abandoned hill? Did they offer words of comfort for Mary and the disciples, or did they continue to mock them with stinging words as they had mocked Jesus?

Sunday

The day dawns bright. But the sun's warmth could not penetrate the cold hand of grief surrounding Mary and the disciples' hearts. They arose to a day they believed would be another one without Jesus. For them, their hope and joy had died on a cross and been sealed in a tomb as dark as their future. Mary went to this tomb to grieve. What was going through Jesus' mind as He waited for the moment when He could reveal Himself to Mary and the others? Was there a twinkle in His eye as He thought of the joy they would soon feel? With heavy heart, Mary walks up to the tomb. The large stone that stood before the tomb's entrance has been moved. She steps inside the tomb that had held Jesus' body since Friday. But now, the tomb is bare, except for an empty shroud. Jesus is no longer there. Then, a vision appears before her. He has risen? Could it possibly be true?

Defeated

In the shadows lurks Satan. The ultimate loser. Humiliated before all the angels. His destiny now sealed. His days of power now numbered. He must get busy to try to salvage something for himself, to gather as many lost souls as he can before his day of destiny comes.

Go tell.

If no one had told, if no one had heard, if no one had believed, the ultimate sacrifice would have been in vain.

Ascension

A home going. Hello Father. Welcome home My Son. I'm very proud of You.

Easter

The word brings so many things to mind: an old rugged cross, suffering, death, resurrection, joy, hope, life. If you will be still and quiet, and listen with your heart, you can hear it - the gentle voice of God saying it all with three simple, heartfelt words, "I love you".

Greater love has no man than this, that a man lay down his life for his friends. John 15:13

A Letter to My Father

My Dear Father,

As I live on this earth, I miss being with You, Father. Sometimes I think back on the beginning days. Together, We created this place called earth. I remember the spectacular display of Your power as You formed the planets and stars. In contrast, I remember Your gentleness as You fashioned the smallest living thing in this world. You used so much care in Your molding of the clay that would become man. You shaped, and flattened, and rounded until this creation was in Our image. I stood there with You as You breathed Your breath into him. Of all Your accomplishments, he was the most treasured.

I'll never forget, Father, the day Your heart broke. There at Your feet lay Your treasured creation, broken and tarnished. What a sad time it was for Us when We had to put man away from Us.

Although it made Us sad, You had already made provision for such an occurrence. Reaching forth Your hand, You set in motion a chain of events that would ultimately lead to where I am right now.

It was hard to leave You, Father. But I love them too, so I kissed You good-bye and slipped into a tiny body. Father, thank you for choosing Mary to be my earthly mother. She is so dear to Me.

These last three years have been exciting times. How special was the day when I asked the woman for a drink from the well. Did You see the surprise in her eyes when I spoke to her? Then, when I offered her a drink from My Living Water, and as understanding came to her, she drank until she was content and whole. I cherish times like those.

Father, I really appreciated the way You multiplied the loaves and fishes so that I could feed all the people there beside the Sea of Galilee. How eagerly did they accept the bread and fish that I broke for them. I wish they would accept as readily My body that soon too will be broken for them.

My time here is coming to an end. Oh, Father, the path before Me will not be an easy one to travel down. They physical pain will be great enough. Having to gaze down at My dear mother as she watches Me die will cut into My heart, much like the spear that will cut into My side. As death slowly makes its temporal claim, I'll be able to see into the hearts of all people, and the rejection I will find in many will break My heart. But, Father, the hardest part will be when You reject Me in Your turning away in order to be able to accept them. Even so, I would do anything, even be separated from You and Your love and enter the depths of hell, to return just one of Your lost sheep to the fold. Each one is so precious to Us.

Father, until that moment comes when You must desert Me for a while, stay close to Me. Help Me to wage the battle that is before Me. When it is over, I'll be waiting for You to breathe Your breath of life into Me.

Let the angels know how much I appreciate their attentiveness to Me. Tell Abraham and Moses that I enjoyed our visit on the Mount.

Abba, Father, I love You. It will be good to come home. I'm really looking forward to being there with You again.

> Your loving Son,
> Jesus

Thanksgiving

Have you ever been on a trip and looked at your map to see just how far you have traveled? When we take time to consider all we have to be thankful for, we are looking at our life map and seeing just how far God has brought us on our journey.

Give Thanks

Thanksgiving is a special time
For thanking God above
For all that He has given
For His abundant love.

He made the world, then filled it
With so many lovely things
Fragrant flowers in the field
And all the birds that sing.

The beauty of a sunset
A soft warm summer night
Newly fallen pure white snow
Reflecting the moonlight.

Then He gave it all to us
To live our lives therein
But we took it all for granted
And ruined it all with sin.

We were left with little hope
And cried out in despair
God heard our cries and then reached out
In His unending care.

Renewing the relationship
That long ago was lost
But the life of His own precious Son
Was the price that it had cost.

(Continued)

Today we pause to look back
On Thanksgivings that have passed
Remembering those loved ones
Who have been called home at last.

Although we miss them deeply
And it makes us all so sad
This is the best Thanksgiving
That they have ever had.

For while we all enjoy a meal
That so lovingly was planned
They share a very special meal
That's served by nail-scarred hands.

And while we're sharing memories
Of days long since gone by
They reminiscence with loved ones
In the dear sweet by and by.

As we reflect on all we have
And family so dear
Let's take a moment to be still
Allowing God to draw us near.

That we might humbly give our thanks
To our Heavenly Father above
For all that He has given
And His unchanging love.

O give thanks to the Lord, for he is good; for his steadfast love endures forever! Psalms 106:1

Christmas

Being lost on a journey is no fun. The miles seem longer. The night seems darker. Then something helps you find your way back to the right road. It might be a map. It might be a road sign. It might be a Star of Bethlehem.

The Joy of Christmas

Christmas. A time of celebration! A time of joy! We sing about it in our Christmas carols - "Hark the Herald Angels Sing", "Joy to the World, the Lord is Come".

Yet, every year there is a part of Christmas that has an element of sadness for me. Come with me back to Bethlehem that first Christmas and I'll show you what I mean.

We come to the stable, the night air still and quiet. As we enter inside, I reach out to feel the rough, coarse wood that was used to form the manger. I'm reminded of another rough, coarse wood that one day will be used to make a cross on a hill.

Look, inside the manger is a precious baby. He has the tiniest hands and such little feet, and the sweetest face. Oh little one, one day they will drive nails through those hands and feet, and press a crown of thorns down on your head until your blood trickles down your face.

I look up at Mary. She sits by the manger, watching her newborn baby sleeping. She is so proud of her firstborn son. You can see the love in her face for Him. I think of how one day she'll have to sit by a cross instead and watch as this her firstborn son dies a cruel, painful death.

I see how Mary has wrapped the baby in swaddling clothes when she laid Him in the manger, and I think of how one day His body will be wrapped in a shroud, and placed in a tomb.

It's almost more than I can bear. I turn away in sadness and in despair, and I wonder, "Where is the joy of Christmas? Why are the angels singing?"

Then, I hear Someone speak to my heart. He says, "Don't be sad. Yes, they drove nails through My hands and feet and they pressed a crown of thorns on My head until blood ran down My face. But they had no power over Me. They could not have done those things except that I allowed it. Don't be sad. Yes, they hung Me on a cross and I died a cruel, painful death. But they could not have taken My life except that I gave it, and I gave it in love for you. Don't be sad. Yes, I was wrapped in a shroud and placed in a tomb. But see, I'm here, right now, just as alive today as I was when I was that little baby, lying in that manger on the first Christmas night."

For me, this is the true meaning, and the true joy of Christmas.

May the God of hope fill you will all joy and peace in believing, so that by the power of the Holy Spirit you may abound in hope.
Romans 15:13

No Christmas Day

I wonder what it would be like
If there was no Christmas Day
If in Bethlehem so long ago
No Babe in the manger lay.

The shepherds keeping loving watch
Over their flocks by night
Would never see the miracle
Of the angels' holy night.

They would not hear the angels' song
About the baby's birth
Or hear them joyously proclaim
Goodwill and peace on earth.

The wise men would not travel
From the Orient afar
For there would be no guiding light
From a brand new Christmas star.

No gold, or myrrh or frankincense
Would the wise men bring
There would be no one to worship
There would be no newborn King.

Mary and Joseph would not hear
This little babe's first cry
She would never sing to Him
Her soft, sweet lullaby.

The world would be so different
The lives of many changed
Compared to what we know today
It all would seem so strange.

There would be no Christmas trees
Decorated with tinsel bright
No carolers singing joyfully
Songs like "Silent Night"

There would be no Christmas cards
With glad tidings we could send
To share our love and happiness
With family and friends.

But most of all there'd be no hope
For you or me today
For there would be no Savior
If there was no Christmas Day.

Happy is he ... whose hope is in the Lord his God. Psalms 146:5

EPILOGUE

Road Map to Heaven

Our experiences in the journey of life started where most journeys start – at the beginning. God starts us on our journey when He gives us the precious gift of life. That journey may be shared with a husband or wife or traveled alone. Each journey crosses paths with the journeys of others. All journeys are known to God, regardless of whether He is invited along on the journey, or if the journey leads down a path away from God.

Each journey through life must end. Some journeys are ended much too soon. For others who are suffering with pain and illness, the journey may seem to go on much too long. Regardless of how or when the journey ends, end it must. We have no choice in that.

Some people think that the journey is all there is. They want to see and do everything along the way, regardless of the paths they may have to take in the process. If the journey leads to nothing, then it really does not matter which path you take. However, the dictionary defines a journey as a passage from one place to another.

The Bible teaches that all journeys end at one of two places – Heaven or hell. Many people think that a loving God would never send anyone to hell. What they forget is that, although a loving God does not want anyone to go to hell, He is also a holy God who must see that justice is satisfied. That means that when we disobey God, then we cannot enter into Heaven, where no disobedience of God is allowed. Justice requires that the penalty for disobedience be paid. The Bible also teaches that we have all disobeyed God, whether in a big way or a small one. Even one disobedient act will close the door to Heaven for that disobedient person.

How can your journey end in Heaven if there is a roadblock of disobedience blocking the entrance for you? You cannot go through it, for it is too solid. You cannot move it out of your way, for it is too heavy. You cannot find a way around it, for it blocks the way completely.

Jesus made a way for us through that roadblock when He died on the cross and then defeated death by coming back to life. Jesus lived on this earth as a man, subject to all the desires of this world, just as you and I. The difference is that He was never disobedient to God. He was willing to experience all the penalties for all of the acts of disobedience ever done by each of us. Why? Because He loves us. He does not love the way we love, which often depends on how we feel or how someone else treats us. He loves us because that is part of His character, regardless of what we do or how we treat Him. Once the penalty owed by us was paid, a way was made through the roadblock to the destination of Heaven.

However, not all journeys end at the destination of Heaven. God gave us the ability to think and choose. He wants us to one day live in Heaven, but He will not force us to go there against our will. Some people want to go to Heaven, but they do not know how to find the right path. They do not know that the Bible is the Road Map to Heaven. Others know that the Bible will tell them the way, but they do not understand how to read the Map. They need someone to help them read the road signs.

> Romans 3:23 (NKJV) says, "For all have sinned and fall short of the glory of God." We have all disobeyed God.

> Ephesians 1:7 (NKJV) states, "In Him, we have redemption through His blood, the forgiveness of sins." Jesus bled and died on the cross in order to pay the penalty we owed and therefore, obtain forgiveness for us.

> Matthew 7:21 (NKJV) points out that "Not everyone who says to me, 'Lord, Lord,' shall enter the kingdom of heaven." Some people think that just because they attend church or believe in the existence of God, they will go to Heaven. Even Satan knows God exists. Something else is needed.

Romans 10:9 (NKJV) tells us, "If you confess with your mouth the Lord Jesus and believe in your heart that God has raised Him from the dead, you will be saved." The moment that we realize that we have disobeyed God and believe that Jesus died in our place, we can ask Him to forgive us and to one day take us to Heaven. That is when He becomes our own personal Savior!

If you are not sure how to ask Him to do be your Savior, you can pray a simple prayer similar to this, "Dear Jesus, I know that I have done things that were disobedient to God. I believe that You died on the cross and then rose from the grave in order to pay the penalty I owe, and thus make it possible for me to be forgiven of those things. Please forgive me and become my Savior. Amen."

Once you do this, you will discover that God will be with you every day to help you in life's struggles and to share with you in life's joys. Your experiences in the journey of life will take on a new meaning, for your journey will now have a sure destination – Heaven.

"I am the Way, the Truth, and the Life . . ." John 14:6